PROCESS
THEOLOGY

PROCESS THEOLOGY

On Postmodernism, Morality, Pluralism, Eschatology, and Demonic Evil

David Ray Griffin

PROCESS CENTURY PRESS
ANOKA, MINNESOTA 2017

Process Theology: On Postmodernism, Morality, Pluralism, Eschatology, and Demonic Evil

Process Century Press
RiverHouse LLC
802 River Lane
Anoka, MN 55303

Process Century Press books are published in association with the International Process Network.

Cover: Susanna Mennicke

VOLUME IV: THEOLOGICAL EXPLORATIONS SERIES
JEANYNE B. SLETTOM, GENERAL EDITOR

ISBN 978-1-940447-30-8
Printed in the United States of America

CONTENTS

SERIES PREFACE: THEOLOGICAL EXPLORATIONS

This series aims to explore the implications of Whiteheadian philosophy and theology for religious belief and practice. It also proposes that process religious thinkers, working from within many different traditions — Buddhist, Confucian, Christian, Hindu, Indigenous, Jewish, Muslim, and others — have unique insights pertinent to the critical issues of our day.

In 1976, we published a book, *Process Theology: An Introductory Exposition,* in which we aimed to "show the creative potentiality of a process perspective in theology." In addition to its explanation of process concepts and their application to Christian doctrine, the book noted the contribution of Whiteheadian thought toward "intercultural and interreligious understanding" and took an early stance on the ecological threat, claiming that process theology was prepared to "make a distinctive contribution" to this challenge.

Since the publication of that book, we have seen many others explore these and other themes in articles, books, and conferences. At the same time, the threat to planetary health and the need for "intercultural and interreligious understanding" has only accelerated. This series is an effort to support theologians and religious philosophers in their ongoing exposition of possible Whiteheadian solutions.

John B. Cobb, Jr.
David Ray Griffin

CHAPTER ONE

Process Theology: Philosophical, Christian, and Postmodern

ALTHOUGH THE LABEL "process theology" is sometimes used more broadly, it usually refers more specifically to the theological movement based primarily on the "process philosophy" of Alfred North Whitehead (1861–1947) and Charles Hartshorne (1897–2000). It is process theology in this more specific sense that is in view here.

Whitehead, after having focused on mathematics and the philosophy of nature in his native England, came in 1924 to Harvard University, where he began developing his metaphysical cosmology. In *Science and the Modern World* (1925), he argued that cosmology should be based on our aesthetic, ethical, and religious intuitions as well as on science. He also argued that developments in science itself were pointing away from mechanistic materialism toward an organismic worldview.

This new worldview led Whitehead, who had earlier been agnostic, to an affirmation, in order to explain the world's order, of the existence of God, understood as the "principle of limitation." In later books—especially *Religion in the Making* (1926), *Process and Reality* (1929), and *Adventures of Ideas* (1933)—Whitehead developed his idea of God far beyond this suggestion of an impersonal principle.

Hartshorne had developed his own philosophical theology before coming under Whitehead's influence as a postdoctoral research fellow at Harvard from 1925 to 1928, during which he served as Whitehead's assistant. But he then adopted most of Whitehead's position, although he maintained his own emphases and even differed with Whitehead on some issues.[1] Hartshorne has given special attention to the idea of God and to arguments for the existence of God, most thoroughly in *The Divine Relativity* (1948) and *Man's Vision of God* (1941), most popularly in *Omnipotence and Other Theological Mistakes* (1984). His overall theistic metaphysics is expressed most comprehensively in *Reality as Social Process* (1953) and *Creative Synthesis and Philosophic Method* (1970). Late in life, Hartshorne reflected back on his life and thought in *The Darkness and the Light: A Philosopher Reflects upon His Fortunate Career and Those Who Made It Possible* (1990).

Because of its employment of Whiteheadian-Hartshornean process philosophy, process theology is one of the few contemporary types of theology to be grounded in a metaphysical position in which theism is defended philosophically, and science and religion are included within the same scheme of thought. In this chapter, I first look at process theology as a natural or philosophical theology, after which I look at specifically Christian process theology.

1 Process Theology as Philosophical Theology

Insofar as "process theology" is an approach shared by theologians of several religious traditions,[2] it is a *natural* theology in the sense of a *philosophical* theology, developing positions that can in principle be accepted by members of many religious traditions. I will discuss five of the dimensions of this philosophical theology.

DIVINE DIPOLARITY AND PERFECTION

One distinctive feature of process theology is its doctrine of divine dipolarity, which contrasts with traditional views of divine "simplicity."

Process theology has, in fact, *two* dipolarities, one emphasized more by Whitehead, the other more by Hartshorne. Whitehead, who distinguished between the "primordial nature" and the "consequent nature" of God, thereby emphasized the distinction between God as *influencing* the world and God as *influenced by* the world.

The primordial nature is God's influence on the world in terms of an appetitive envisagement of the primordial potentialities ("eternal objects") for finite realization. This is God as the Divine Eros (which Nikos Kazantzakis called the Divine Cry),[3] who lures the world forward with a vision of novel possibilities. The consequent nature is God as affected by and responsive to the world.

The second dipolarity, emphasized by Hartshorne's distinction between God's "abstract essence" and "concrete states," is a distinction between God as *unchanging* and God as *changing*, respectively.

God's abstract essence has most of the attributes given to God as a whole by classical theism — immutability, impassibility, eternity, and independence — leading Hartshorne to refer to his doctrine as "neo-classical theism."[4] But this immutable essence is a mere abstraction from God. God as concrete is, for Hartshorne as for Whitehead, God as interacting creatively and responsively with the world.

Whereas classical theism, following Greek philosophy, equated perfection with completeness and therefore immutability, Hartshorne argued that we must think of God in terms of two kinds of perfection. God's abstract essence exemplifies the *unchanging* type of perfection. For example, to say that God is omniscient is to say that God always knows everything knowable; this abstract feature of God does not change.

But God's concrete knowledge does change because, given the ultimate reality of process, new things are always happening and thereby becoming knowable. God's concrete states thereby exemplify the *relative* type of perfection, a perfection that can be surpassed. Of course, God in one moment is surpassable by no creature but only by God in a later moment.

The same distinction can be made with regard to other attributes. For example, God at every moment loves all creatures perfectly, wishing them all well and feeling their experiences sympathetically—suffering with their pains, rejoicing with their joys. To say that God grows is to say not that God becomes wiser or more loving but only that, as new creatures arise and new experiences occur, the objects of the divine love have increased and therefore the divine experience has been enriched.

NATURALISTIC THEISM AND THE PROBLEM OF EVIL

Process theism is a naturalistic theism. It is naturalistic not in the sense of equating God with "nature" or otherwise denying distinct agency to God, but simply in the sense of rejecting supernaturalism, understood as the doctrine of a divine being that can interrupt the world's normal causal principles.

This rejection is rooted in process theology's view of the relation of God to being itself, which it renames "creativity" to reflect the fact that that which all beings embody is not passive stuff but dynamic energy. Creativity, more precisely, is each actuality's twofold power to exercise a modicum of self-determination (final causation) and then to exert influence (efficient causation) on future actualities.

Traditional theism, with its ontotheological equation of God with being itself, said that this twofold power is essentially embodied in God alone. Because any power possessed by creatures was a gift, the normal causal patterns among creatures could be interrupted at any time. This position was fully enunciated only with the post-biblical development of the doctrine of creation *ex nihilo*.[5]

Process theologians return to the view—common to Plato, the Bible, and Christian thinkers prior to the end of second century—that our universe was created by God's bringing a particular type of order out of chaos.[6] For process theologians, an essential implication of this idea is that creative power is essentially embodied in a world of finite actualities as well as in the divine actuality.

The divine power, accordingly, is necessarily persuasive: It could not be coercive or controlling in the sense of unilaterally determining what happens in the world. This view of the God-world relation therefore reconciles theism with the scientific community's naturalistic assumption that no events, however extraordinary, involve violations of the world's basic causal principles."[7]

To emphasize the idea that the world is both intimately related to and yet distinct from God, process theologians sometimes, with Hartshorne, refer to their position as "panentheism." This term, which means that "all (finite) things are in God," signals process theism's difference from traditional theism's insistence that God could (and perhaps once upon a time did) exist all alone, without a world of finite actualities. The term panentheism emphasizes the idea that the existence of a world is internal to God—that it belongs to the very nature of God to be in relation to a world. What exists necessarily is not simply God but God-with-a-world. In contrast with pantheism, however, panentheism says that both God and the world have their own creativity, their own power, so that the evils in the world do not betoken evil or even imperfection in God.[8]

This view also provides the basis for a theodicy that defends the perfect goodness of our creator without minimizing the evil of our world. The distinction between God and creativity provides, in fact, the basis for a robust doctrine of demonic evil, with the basic idea being that God's creation of human beings brought into existence a level of worldly creativity that not only could become diametrically opposed to the divine creativity but could also do so with sufficient power to threaten divine purposes.[9]

But that doctrine of the demonic is simply an extreme implication of the more general point, which is that God's power is misconstrued if it is thought to be all-controlling power. Against traditional all-determining theism, affirmed by Augustine, Thomas, Calvin, and Luther, process theologians deny that God determines everything that happens in the world.[10] And against traditional free-will theologians, process theologians deny that God *could* control all events but refuses to prevent evil in order to allow human freedom.[11]

Process theologians say, instead, that the creation has its own creativity and hence its own inherent power. Also, in bringing forth more complex creatures, such as multicelled animals and especially human beings, God necessarily brought forth creatures with *more* creativity and hence more of the twofold power to exercise self-determination and causal influence on others. These higher creatures are, accordingly, necessarily more dangerous. Even God cannot have the greater good without the risk of the greater evil. Given this view of the God-world relation, the realization that our world is filled with horrendous evils need not lead to atheism.

CREATION AND EVOLUTION

The insistence that God does not have coercive, controlling power does not mean, however, that God does not act creatively and providentially in the world. God is the creator of our world. Both the novelty in and the directionality of the evolutionary process, through which our present world was created out of a chaotic state involving nothing but extremely trivial events, are explained through God's creative-providential activity.

One key to Whitehead's reconciliation of creation and evolution is his rejection of the materialistic, mechanistic view of nature, according to which it is composed of bits of matter that can only be affected externally, by other bits of matter. He instead, with his panexperientialism, portrays the ultimate units of nature as *experiential events*, each of which "prehends" other events, taking influences from them into itself. Each unitary event prehends, thereby being internally constituted by, influences from everything in its environment.

Given a panentheistic worldview, this environment includes not only other finite events but also the all-pervasive influence of God. This divine influence is the source of both the order and the ever-arising novelty in the world. Because different forms of novelty are relevant in different events, this divine influence is variable in content. But this variable divine influence does not contradict the idea that process theism is *naturalistic*, because this divine influence, with its variableness, is a natural part of the normal causal processes of the world, never an interruption of them. The widespread assumption among evolutionists that naturalism requires atheism, or at least deism, is shown to be untrue. Naturalism is fully compatible with panentheism.[12]

From this perspective, there is no reason to accept the neo-Darwinian assumption that the evolutionary process must have proceeded without any cosmic directivity. However, process theologians agree with the main Darwinian point, that no species have been created *ex nihilo*. But they do not accept the much stronger claim that new species arise purely from the combined effect of random variations and natural selection, which amounts to the claim that the direction of the evolutionary process is explainable without appeal to any nonlocal influence. Given a naturalistic theism in which divine influence involves the suggestion of possible new forms of existence, which operate as "attractors," we can understand why evolution (evidently) proceeded by means of a series of leaps, rather than very tiny steps (as neo-Darwinism requires), and why the process has led, at least in some lines, to increasingly greater complexity, which produces increasingly richer forms of experience.[13]

RELIGIOUS PLURALISM

The distinction between God and creativity has also been employed by process theologians to develop a version of religious pluralism that can regard theistic and nontheistic religious experiences as equally veridical. Theistic religious experience, which leads the experiencers to think of ultimate reality as a personal being who loves the world, is an experience of God. Nontheistic religious experience, insofar as it leads some Hindus to speak of "nirguna Brahman" and some Buddhists to speak of "emptiness," is an experience of creativity. This position means giving up the old idea that there is only one ultimate reality. Process theologians speak, instead, of God as the *personal* ultimate and of creativity as the *impersonal* ultimate.

This more pluralistic view of ideas about ultimate reality is correlated with a more pluralistic idea of salvation. Rather than holding, as do many pluralists, that the various religions promote basically the same kind of salvation, Whiteheadians argue that different religions promote different types of salvation—different types of "wholeness."[14]

ECOLOGICAL AND FEMINIST THEOLOGY

One of the features of process theology that has made it especially attractive to many people in recent decades is the fact that it provides the basis for a deeply ecological theology. Given its panexperientialism, it rejects the traditional and early modern dualism between humanity and nature, which assigned intrinsic value only to human beings.

According to process theology, all genuine individuals have intrinsic value, meaning value for themselves. God did not, anthropocentrists to the contrary, create "nature" simply as a backdrop for the divine-human drama, and certainly not for human plunder. God cherishes individuals of each kind for their own sakes. However, unlike egalitarian versions of deep ecology, process theology does not say that all individuals have the *same degree* of intrinsic value. A chimpanzee has more intrinsic value than a microbe, a human more than a chimpanzee. A basis is thereby provided for discriminating value judgments.[15]

In spite of its affirmation of a hierarchy of intrinsic values, however, process theology has a way of recognizing an element of truth in the egalitarian idea that all things have equal value. Besides intrinsic value, all things also have extrinsic value, one very important dimension of which is their ecological value—their value for sustaining the ecological system. And those things with the most intrinsic value generally have the least ecological value. So, when we consider the *total* value of each species, we can say that, roughly speaking, all things have equal value.[16]

Recognition of the hierarchy of intrinsic value does not, therefore, lead to the conclusion that species with less intrinsic value should be eliminated to make room for increased populations of those with greater intrinsic value. With its dual emphasis on intrinsic and extrinsic value, process theology reinforces respect and care both for individual animals — the respect that lies behind the humane society and the animal liberation movement — and for the ecological system as a whole — the respect that inspires deep ecologists and the earth liberation movement.

Many features of process theology have made it attractive to feminist theologians. As illustrated by the writings of Catherine Keller, Nancy Howell, and Carol Christ,[17] these features include process theology's emphasis on internal relations, its view that divine power is persuasive rather than coercive, and its conviction that the divine reality is responsive to and inclusive of the world — all of which cut against portraying the divine and the human in stereotypically masculine terms.

The fact that process theology provides support for feminist concerns is arguably one of its most important features. Process theologian John Cobb, for example, has said: "Culturally and intellectually, the most important movement of the twentieth century may prove to have been feminism."[18] In any case, given the point of the prior paragraph, the form of feminism that process theology supports most strongly is ecofeminism.[19]

2 Process Theology as Distinctively Christian Theology

Although there are process theologians who belong to other traditions, most process theologians thus far have been Christians. And although they typically spend much of their time on the philosophical doctrines of process theology, they also use those doctrines to deal with distinctively Christian themes. I will illustrate this side of Christian process theology with its treatment of trinitarianism, christology, and salvation.

GOD AS TRINITARIAN

The idea that God both affects the world and is responsive to the world is sometimes made in terms of a distinction between God's "creative love" and God's "responsive love."[20] With this distinction, we would have only a binitarian, not a trinitarian, doctrine. But process theology, besides distinguishing between God and creativity, also says that God is the primordial *embodiment* of creativity. We must distinguish, in other words, between creativity as embodied in God—*divine creativity*—and creativity as embodied in the world—*creaturely creativity*. Divine creativity differs from creaturely creativity by virtue of always being perfectly qualified by creative and responsive love. In other words, God's outgoing creativity is always aimed at promoting the greatest possible good for the creatures, while God's responsive creativity is always characterized by perfect compassion for the creatures. The divine threefoldness can hence be understood as consisting of divine creativity, creative love, and responsive love.

Besides suggesting such an "immanent" trinitarianism, according to which God is internally threefold, process theology also suggests an "economic" trinitarianism, according to which there is a threefoldness in the way in which God is manifest in the world. One economic trinity endorsed by process theologians focuses on God as creator, redeeming revealer, and sanctifier. According to the Nicene Creed, the divine reality that was incarnate in Jesus is as fully divine as the world's creator. The Council of Constantinople extended this point to the Holy Spirit. Christian process theologians can interpret these affirmations to mean that the way God as Holy Spirit acts in relation to human experience generally—by persuasion—is the same way in which God acted in creating the world and in becoming revealingly incarnate in Jesus.[21]

INCARNATIONAL CHRISTOLOGY

Having already discussed creation through persuasion, I will here discuss how God, working persuasively, could have been present in

Jesus in a way that makes it appropriate for Christians to continue looking to him for their basic clue about the character of our creator.

Given process philosophy's understanding of causation and perception, this kind of incarnation could have resulted from Jesus' experience of—his prehensions of—God's influence on him. Causation between two individuals does not involve an external relation, like the impact of one billiard ball on another, but involves an internal relation, in which the cause enters into the effect.

Whitehead's philosophy, he said, "is mainly devoted to the task of making clear the notion of 'being present in another entity.'"[22] In application to God, this point means that, because God influences all events, God is present in all events. Whitehead even said that "the world lives by its incarnation of God in itself."[23] Within this framework, then, there is no problem of understanding how God could have been incarnate in Jesus. The only question is how God could have been present in such a way as to make Jesus a decisive revelation of God.

Process theology can answer this question in terms of five points.

- First, God always presents initial aims toward the best possibilities open to the individual, given its past history and present situation. These initial aims constitute prevenient grace.

- Second, the best possibilities for different individuals can differ radically. For example, the best possibilities for a human being differ radically from the best possibilities for electrons or mice, and the best possibilities for a first-century Jew differed greatly from the best possibilities open to a Buddhist in India at the time. The nature of the divine aims and therefore the prevenient grace for different individuals will, therefore, differ radically.

- Third, the aims for some individuals will reflect the general divine aim more directly than the aims for other individuals.

- Fourth, assuming that the history of Israel, including especially the messages of the prophets, involved genuine revelation of the divine will, a devout person such as Jesus, growing up in that tradition, would be well suited to receive divine aims highly reflective of the general aim of God for the world, especially the human world.

• Fifth, we can understand Jesus as one in whom God was incarnate in such a way that it is appropriate for us to apprehend Jesus as a decisive revelation of God's character, purpose, and mode of operation.[24]

SALVATION

The good news proclaimed by Jesus evidently involved salvation in a threefold sense. His message revolved around the idea of a Reign of God on earth, in which, as the prayer he taught his disciples said, God's will would be done on earth, which would mean, among other things, that everyone would have their "daily bread." Jesus also referred to salvation in a life beyond bodily death. And Jesus presupposed, thirdly, that our present life is everlastingly meaningful because it is known by God. Process theologians can affirm all three of these dimensions.

With regard to the third dimension, the doctrine of God's responsive love means that our present activities are received into God with compassion and remembered everlastingly. The threat of meaninglessness posed by modern atheism is hence overcome. All process theologians affirm salvation in this sense. Indeed, because some process theologians have, following Hartshorne, affirmed salvation *only* in this sense,[25] it is sometimes thought that this is the only sense in which process theologians affirm salvation.

But process philosophy, as Whitehead himself pointed out, allows for the possibility that the human soul can live on apart from the physical body. And some process theologians have, on the basis of this ontological possibility combined with empirical evidence and faith in divine grace, affirmed the reality of a "resurrection of the soul."[26] This affirmation can then provide the basis for hope for a process of sanctification, in which God will gradually love the hell out of us.[27]

Thirdly, the idea of a reign of God on earth has also been developed from the process point of view. The next major evolutionary leap towards which the creative love of God is luring us is arguably global democracy, in which the war system, with its inevitable imperialism and terrorism, is replaced by democratic rule at the global level, through which the rights and interests of all peoples would be protected and the common good promoted.

Such a political reorganization would provide the most crucial necessary condition for a form of social-political-economic governance in which divine values — truth, justice, equality, compassion, peace, and ecological sustainability — replace the demonic values in terms of which the planet has increasingly been ruled since the rise of the war-system some 10,000 years ago.[28]

Salvation in this sense entails thinking of "process theology as political theology" and/or as liberation theology.[29]

Notes

1   Lewis S. Ford, ed., *Two Process Philosophers: Hartshorne's Encounter with Whitehead* (American Academy of Religion, 1973).

2   David Ray Griffin, ed., *Deep Religious Pluralism* (Westminster/John Knox, 2005).

3   Nikos Kazantzakis, *Report to Greco*, trans. P. A. Bien (Simon & Schuster, 1965), 291–92.

4   Schubert M. Ogden, "Christian Theology and Neoclasssical Theism," *Journal of Religion*, April 1980.

5   See Chapter 6, "Process Theodicy and Climate Change."

6   Catherine Keller, *The Face of the Deep: A Theology of Becoming* (Routledge, 2002).

7   David Ray Griffin, *Two Great Truths: A New Synthesis of Scientific Naturalism and Christian Faith* (Westminster John Knox Press, 2004).

8   *Panentheism and Scientific Naturalism: Rethinking Evil, Morality,*

Religious Experience, Religious Pluralism, and the Academic Study of Religion (Process Century Press, 2014).

9 See Chapter 7, "Divine Goodness and Demonic Evil."

10 Thomas Jay Oord, *The Uncontrolling Love of God: An Open and Relational Account of Providence* (IVP Academic, 2015).

11 See Chapter 5, "Can a Traditional Free-Will Theodicy Be Adequate after All?" David Ray Griffin, *Evil Revisited: Responses and Reconsiderations* (State University of New York Press, 1991); Griffin, "Process Theology and the Christian Good News: A Response to Classical Free Will Theism," in John B. Cobb, Jr., and Clark H. Pinnock, eds., *Searching for an Adequate God: A Dialogue between Process and Free Will Theists* (Eerdmans, 2000), 1–38.

12 See Chapter 3, "Evolution," in David Ray Griffin, *God Exists but Gawd Does Not: From Evil to New Atheism to Fine-Tuning* (Process Century Press, 2016).

13 See David Ray Griffin, "Neo-Darwinism and its Religious Implications," in Griffin, *Harmonizing Science and Religion: Essays in Process Thought* (Process Century Press, 2017); for a more extensive treatment, see "Creation and Evolution," Chapter 8 of Griffin, *Religion and Scientific Naturalism: Overcoming the Conflicts* (State University of New York Press, 2000).

14 John B. Cobb, Jr., *Beyond Dialogue: Toward a Mutual Transformation of Buddhism and Christianity* (Fortress, 1982), and Cobb, *Transforming Christianity and the World: A Way beyond Absolutism and Relativism*, ed. Paul F. Knitter (Orbis Books, 1999); Marjorie Hewitt Suchocki, *Divinity & Diversity: A Christian Affirmation of Religious Pluralism* (Abingdon, 2003); David Ray Griffin, *Deep Religious Pluralism* (Westminster/John Knox, 2005).

15 John B. Cobb, Jr., *Is It Too Late? A Theology of Ecology* (1972; revised ed., Environmental Ethics Books, 1995); Jay B. McDaniel, *Of God and Pelicans: A Theology of Reverence for Life* (John Knox, 1989) and *Earth, Sky, Gods, & Mortals: Developing an Ecological Spiritusality* Twenty-Third Publcations, 1990; Charles Birch, *Regaining Compassion for Humanity and* Nature (New South Wales University Press, 1993; Chalice Press, 1993).

16 "Whitehead's Deeply Ecological Worldview," Chapter 4 of Griffin,

Whitehead's Radically Different Postmodern Philosophy: An Argument for Its Contemporary Relevance (State University of New York Press, 2007).

17 Catherine Keller, *From a Broken Web: Separation, Sexism and Self* (Beacon Press, 1986); Nancy Howell, *A Feminist Cosmology: Ecology, Solidarity, and Metaphysics* (Humanity, 2000); Carol P. Christ, *She Who Changes: Re-Imagining the Divine in the World* (Palgrave, 2003); *Goddess and God in the World: Conversations in Embodied Theology* (Fortress Press, 2016).

18 John B. Cobb, Jr., *Postmodernism and Public Policy: Reframing Religion, Culture, Education, Sexuality, Class, Race, Politics, and the Economy* (State University of New York Press, 2002).

19 Rosemary Radford Ruether, *Gaia and God: An Ecofeminist Theology of Earth Healing* (HarperCollins, 1994).

20 See Chapter 3, "God as Creative-Responsive Love," in John B. Cobb, Jr., and David Ray Griffin, *Process Theology: An Introductory Exposition* (Westminster Press, 1976).

21 See "Christian Faith: From Arrogance to Timidity to Respectful Confidence," Chapter 4 of Griffin, *Two Great Truths: A New Synthesis of Scientific Naturalism and Christian Faith* (Westminster John Knox Press, 2004).

22 Alfred North Whitehead, *Process and Reality* (1929), corrected edition, ed. David Ray Griffin and Donald W. Sherburne (Free Press, 1978), 50.

23 Alfred North Whitehead, *Religion in the Making* (1926, Macmillan; Fordham University Press, 1996), 156.

24 David R. Griffin, *A Process Christology* (Westminster, 1973; reprinted with new preface, University Press of America, 1990); "Jesus Christ," Chapter 6 of Cobb and Griffin, *Process Theology*; John B. Cobb, Jr., *Christ in a Pluralistic Age* (Westminster, 1975).

25 For example, Schubert M. Ogden, *The Reality of God and Other Essays* (Harper & Row, 1966).

26 John B. Cobb, Jr., "The Resurrection of the Soul," *Harvard Theological Review*, April 1987: 213–27).

27 David Ray Griffin, *Parapsychology, Philosophy, and Spirituality: A*

Postmodern Exploration (State University of New York Press, 1997; Griffin, *Two Great Truths*; Marjorie Hewitt Suchocki, *The End of Evil: Process Eschatology in Historical Context* (State University of New York Press, 1988).

28   David Ray Griffin, "The Moral Need for Global Democracy," *Belonging Together: Faith and Politics in a Relational World*, ed. Douglas Sturm (Claremont: P&F Press, 2003: 119–39).

29   John B. Cobb, Jr., *Process Theology as Political Theology* (Westminster, 1982); C. Robert Mesle, *Process Theology: A Basic Introduction* (Chalice Press, 1993), 65–68, 75–80; Henry J. Young, *Hope in Process: A Theology of Social Pluralism* (Fortress Press, 1991); David Ray Griffin, "Postmodern Theology as First-World Liberation Theology," in *Religion and the Postmodern Vision: Paine Lectures 1991* (University of Missouri-Columbia, 1992), 1–22.

CHAPTER TWO

Reconstructive Postmodern Theology

RECONSTRUCTIVE POSTMODERN THEOLOGY DERIVES ITS philosophical bearings from the movement in which Alfred North Whitehead is the central figure, with William James and Charles Hartshorne being, respectively, the most important antecedent and subsequent members. Although theology based on this movement has widely been known as "process theology," not all process theology is properly called postmodern. Process theology *is* reconstructive postmodern theology insofar as it thematizes the contrast between the modern and the postmodern, emphasizes the distinctively postmodern notions in Whiteheadian philosophy, employs these notions for deconstruction of classical and modern concepts and for ensuing reconstruction, and relates the resulting position to other forms of postmodern thought. Although this form of postmodern thought has generally been called "constructive," as in the title of my State University of New York (SUNY) Series in Constructive Postmodern Thought, the term "reconstructive" makes clearer that a prior deconstruction of received concepts is presupposed.

1 Origins

Although the term "postmodern" was not used by Whitehead himself, the notion was implicit in his 1925 book, *Science and the Modern World*, in which he said that recent developments in both physics and philosophy have superseded some of the scientific and philosophical ideas that were foundational for the modern world.

Whitehead's most explicit statement about the end of the modern epoch occurred in a discussion of William James's 1904 essay "Does Consciousness Exist," the crux of which Whitehead took to be the denial that consciousness is *a stuff that is essentially different from the stuff of which the physical world is composed*. Whitehead suggested that just as Descartes, with his formulation of a dualism between matter and mind, could (with some exaggeration) be regarded as the thinker who inaugurated the modern period, James, with his challenge to Cartesian dualism, could (with similar exaggeration) be regarded as having inaugurated "a new stage in philosophy."

Viewing this challenge together with that offered to "scientific materialism" by physics in the same period, Whitehead suggested that this "double challenge marks the end of a period which lasted for about two hundred and fifty years."[1] Having described the scientific and philosophical thought of that period as distinctively modern, Whitehead thereby implied that his own philosophy, which sought to unite the philosophical implications of relativity and quantum physics with the Jamesian rejection of dualism, was distinctively postmodern.

The term itself was applied to Whitehead's philosophy in a 1964 essay by John B. Cobb, Jr., entitled "From Crisis Theology to the Post-Modern World," which dealt with the emerging discussion of the "Death of God."[2] Arguing that the dominant modern mentality (which equates the real with the objects of sensory perception) excludes the possible causality and even reality of God, thereby leading to relativism and nihilism, Cobb portrayed Whitehead's philosophy as distinctively postmodern by virtue of the fact that his epistemology rejected the primacy of sense perception, that his ontology replaced material substances with events having intrinsic value and internal relations, and that he developed these ideas by reflecting on problems in modern science.

In *God and the World* (1967) and "The Possibility of Theism Today" (1968), Cobb restated his argument that Whitehead provided a postmodern vision in which theology is again possible.[3] These writings provided the stimulus for my decision in 1972, as co-editor of a volume on Cobb's theology (which did not actually appear until 1977), to orient my introductory essay around the notion that Cobb was providing a "Post-Modern Theology for a New Christian Existence."[4] In Cobb's 1975 book, *Christ in a Pluralistic Age*, he enlarged his use of the term "postmodern," employing it to refer to a pluralistic method and mindset that goes beyond the idea of a single truth without falling into complete relativism.[5]

Cobb was not the only one who was thinking of Whitehead's philosophy as postmodern. In the same year as Cobb's seminal essay (1964), Floyd Matson, who was also influenced by Whitehead, advocated a "postmodern science," by which he meant one that overcame mechanistic, reductionistic, and behaviorist approaches.[6] In 1973, a "post-modern science" was advocated at greater length and with more explication of Whitehead's position by Harold Schilling.[7] In that same year, Charles Altieri argued that it was Whitehead's philosophy, even more than Heidegger's, that best explains the connection between fact and value suggested by a number of American poets considered distinctively postmodern by Altieri.[8] In a 1976 book subtitled *Resources for the Post-Modern World*, Frederick Ferré, besides following Schilling in speaking of the need for the kind of "post-modern science" provided by Whitehead, also suggested that Christian process theology presents a "post-modern version of Christianity" that could help overcome the ecological crisis engendered by modernity.[9]

While at Cambridge University in 1980, I gave a lecture, in the form of a response to John Hick's *The Myth of God Incarnate*,[10] entitled

"Myth, Incarnation, and the Need for a Postmodern Theology."
Arguing that we need "a postmodern outlook [that] would preserve
the unquestionable advances made by the tenets of modernity, but
relativize some of them by placing them within the context of a more
inclusive understanding, somewhat as Newtonian physics is included
in, but modified by, 20th-century physics," I added:

> Cambridge's own Alfred North Whitehead has provided a
> philosophic vision that can be called postmodern and does
> make possible the kind of theology that is necessary in our
> time.[11]

Three years later I founded the Center for a Postmodern World (in
Santa Barbara, California). Its invited lectures and its 1987 conference,
"Toward a Postmodern World," provided most of the material for
the three books that launched the SUNY Series in Constructive
Postmodern Thought.[12]

Through the influence of this center and book series, a circle
of reconstructive postmodern thinkers was formed, some of whom
were involved in distinctively Christian thinking, including—besides
Cobb, Ferré, and myself—New Testament scholar William Beardslee,
biologist Charles Birch, economist Herman Daly, and feminist
theologian Catherine Keller.

Having long considered 1964 the year in which the term postmodern began to be applied to the Whiteheadian approach, I
subsequently learned that this application had actually been made
as early as 1944, when John Herman Randall, Jr., writing of the
emergence of "'post-modern' naturalistic philosophies," referred to
Whitehead as "one of the pioneers" of this movement.[13]

The great advantage of this postmodern naturalism, said
Randall, is that by rejecting the modern, mechanistic, reductionistic
type of naturalism, it overcomes the modern conflict of scientific
naturalism with moral, aesthetic, and religious values—a description
that accords completely with the stated purpose of Whitehead's
philosophy.[14]

In any case, whether the use of the term "postmodern" to refer to a Whiteheadian approach is said to have begun in 1964 or 1944, it is ironic that some critics, understanding the term in light of meanings it took on in the 1980s, have considered the Whiteheadian use of the term opportunistic. It is noteworthy that in a 1995 volume on "early postmodernism" in which Altieri's 1973 article was reprinted,[15] the editor's introduction draws attention to the great difference between this early "postmodernism" and the type of thought with which the name later became associated. The task of the present essay, in any event, is to explain not only what the Whiteheadian type of postmodern theology says but why its advocates consider it genuinely postmodern.

2 The Questions of Metaphysics and Rationality

The fact that reconstructive postmodern theology is based on a metaphysical type of philosophy makes it distinctive, given the fact that "metaphysics" is one of the things that most other forms of postmodernism believe we now are, or should be, beyond. This difference is to some extent terminological, in that many of the definitions of metaphysics that are presupposed in this widespread rejection do not apply to Whitehead's thought.

- Many postmodernists, for example, presuppose the Kantian conception, according to which metaphysics is the attempt to talk about things beyond all possible experience, whereas Whitehead understands it as the endeavor to construct a coherent scheme of ideas "in terms of which every element of our experience can be interpreted," adding that the "elucidation of immediate experience is the sole justification for any thought."[16]

- Sometimes metaphysics is understood as an approach that necessarily does violence to experience for the sake of a tidy system, but Whitehead, who praised the intellectual life of

William James for being one long "protest against the dismissal of experience in the interest of system,"[17] insisted repeatedly on the need to consider the "whole of the evidence" and *every* type of experience, insisting: "Nothing can be omitted."[18]

- Thinkers influenced by Heidegger sometimes portray metaphysics as necessarily committed to the domination of nature, but Whitehead's metaphysical analysis led him to say that our experience of actuality is "a value experience. Its basic expression is—Have a care, here is something that matters!"[19]

- Still another reason for rejecting metaphysical systems is that they claim to attain certainty, but Whitehead regarded a metaphysical system as a tentative hypothesis, an "experimental adventure," adding that "the merest hint of dogmatic certainty as to finality of statement is an exhibition of folly."[20]

- Closely related is the widespread assumption that metaphysics is necessarily "foundationalist" in the sense now widely discredited, according to which the philosopher begins with a few indubitable basic beliefs, from which all other beliefs are deduced. But Whitehead explicitly rejected the idea "that metaphysical thought started from principles which were individually clear, distinct, and certain."[21]

However, although many of the apparent differences between Whiteheadians and other types of postmodernists can be dismissed in these ways, a real difference remains. Reconstructive postmodernism is oriented around the conviction that we must and can reconcile religion and reason, which in our time largely means religion and science. Whitehead, in fact, said that philosophy's most important task is to show how religion and the sciences (natural and social) can be integrated into a coherent worldview.[22]

Other postmodernists, by contrast, reject *any* attempt at a comprehensive account of things, whether the attempt be called a metanarrative, metaphysics, or something else, considering all such attempts to be ideological efforts to impose one's will on others. But Whiteheadian postmodernists, while recognizing that every such attempt will involve distortions due to ignorance and bias, deny that the very effort to engage in comprehensive thinking necessarily involves hegemonial intentions.[23] They argue, furthermore, that the human need for stories or narratives orienting us to reality as a whole cannot be removed by declaration.[24]

The differences here involve fundamentally different ideas about modernity's fatal flaw. While these other postmodernists see modernity as afflicted by rationalistic pretensions, Whitehead regarded modernity as an essentially *anti*-rational enterprise. His point depends on the idea that beliefs that we inevitably presume in practice should be taken as the ultimate criteria for rational thought. "Rationalism," said Whitehead, "is the search for the coherence of such presumptions."[25]

A precedent-setting instance of modern anti-rationalism was Hume's acknowledgment that in living he necessarily presupposed various ideas, such as a real world and causal influence, that could find no place in his philosophy. Whitehead argued that rather than resting content with a philosophical theory that had to be supplemented by an appeal to "practice," Hume should have revised his philosophy until it included all the inevitable presuppositions of practice.[26]

The reason that it is anti-rational to deny in theory ideas that are necessarily presupposed in practice is that one thereby violates the first rule of reason, the law of noncontradiction, because one is simultaneously denying (explicitly) and affirming (implicitly) the idea in question.

3 Overcoming Problematic Modern Assumptions

From the reconstructive postmodern perspective, it lies at the heart of the task of postmodern thinking to overcome the assumptions that led to the modern dualism between the ideas affirmed in theory and those presupposed in practice. The crucial assumptions are taken to be:

- The *sensationist view of perception*, according to which our sensory organs provide our only means of perceiving things beyond ourselves.

- The *mechanistic view of nature*, according to which the ultimate units of nature are devoid of all experience, intrinsic value, internal purpose, and internal relations.

It was these correlative ideas that led to the modern divorce of theoretical from practical reason and thereby to the Humean-Kantian conviction that metaphysics, which would show how the two sets of ideas can be integrated into a self-consistent worldview, is impossible.

THE SENSATIONIST DOCTRINE OF PERCEPTION

The sensationist doctrine of perception is responsible for many of the problems, including those involving causation, a real world, and a real past.

Causation

With regard to causation, Hume famously pointed out that although we have usually thought of causation as involving some sort of *necessary connection* between the cause and the effect, because the "cause" is thought to exert *real influence* on the "effect," sensory data provide no basis for this idea, so that causation, to be an empirical concept, must be redefined to mean simply *constant correlation* between two types of events. Although Hume continued to presuppose in practice that causation involves real influence—that his wine glass moved to his lips because he used his hand to lift it—he said that *qua* philosopher he could not employ that meaning.

Reality of the World

Hume even said that he as philosopher could not affirm the reality of the world. He could not help, he pointed out, being a realist in everyday life, necessarily presupposing that he lived in a world with other people and things, such as tables and food. According to his analysis of perception, however, he did not perceive such things but only sense data, such as colors and shapes. As a philosopher, therefore, he had to be a solipsist, doubting the existence of an external world, even though in practice, including the practice of using a pen to record his skeptical ideas on paper, he had no doubts.

Reality of Time and the Past

At the outset of the twentieth century, George Santayana showed that the Humean brand of empiricism leads not simply to solipsism but to "solipsism of the present moment."[27] Because sense perception reveals only various data immediately present to our consciousness, we must be agnostic about the reality of the past and therefore of time.

Empiricist philosophy was said, accordingly, to be unable to support four of the most fundamental presuppositions of the empirical sciences — the reality of causal influence, time, the past, and even the world as such. Having no basis for saying that causal relations observed in the past will hold true in the future, this kind of empiricist philosophy obviously could not justify the principle of scientific induction. Much postmodernism has drawn the conclusion that science, generally taken to be the paradigm of rationality, is itself rationally groundless.

Normative Values

The sensationist version of empiricism leads to the same conclusion about normative values. Philosophers had traditionally affirmed the existence of logical, aesthetic, and moral norms. Sensory perception, however, can provide no access to such norms. Early modern philosophers, such as John Locke and Francis Hutcheson, said that we know such norms because they were divinely revealed or implanted in our minds. But late modernity, having rejected supernatural explanations, concluded that all such norms are our own creations.

Most forms of postmodernism have emphasized the implications of this conclusion, saying that we must regard even our most basic moral convictions as local conventions with no rational grounding—even while continuing to presuppose, in the very act of writing such things, that various moral norms, such as the idea that we should not repress "difference" and oppress the "other," are universally valid. The apparent necessity to presuppose various ideas even while criticizing them is sometimes justified by referring to them as "transcendental illusions" in the Kantian sense.

4 Whitehead's Alternative View of Perception

Whiteheadian postmodernism, rather than accepting the inevitability of such contradictions, follows James's "radical empiricism" in rejecting the sensationist view of perception. At the heart of Whitehead's epistemology is his deconstruction of sensory perception, showing that it is a hybrid composed of two pure modes of perception. Hume and most subsequent philosophy noticed only "perception in the mode of presentational immediacy," in which sense data are immediately present to the mind. If this were our only mode of perception, we would indeed be doomed to solipsism of the present moment.

But this mode of perception, Whitehead argued at great length—much of *Process and reality* and virtually all of *Symbolism*[28] are devoted to this point—is derivative from a more fundamental mode, "perception in the mode of causal efficacy," through which we directly perceive other actualities as exerting causal efficacy upon ourselves—which explains why we know that other actualities exist and that causation is more than constant conjunction. One example of this mode of perception, which Whitehead also calls "prehension," is the prehension of our own sensory organs as causing us to have certain experiences, as when we are aware that we are seeing a tree *by means of* our eyes. Such prehension, while presupposed in sensory perception, is itself nonsensory.

Another example of this nonsensory perception is our prehension of prior moments of our own experience, through which we know the reality of the past and thereby of time. This point depends on a third idea deconstructed by Whitehead—the idea, common to modern and premodern Western thought (although rejected long ago by Buddhists), that enduring individuals are "substances," with a "substance" understood to be both actual and not analyzable into entities that are more fully actual.

According to Whitehead's alternative account, an individual that endures through time, such as an electron, a living cell, or a human soul, is analyzable into momentary actual entities, which he called "actual occasions." To remember a previous moment of one's own experience, therefore, is to prehend an actual entity that is numerically different from the actual occasion that is one's present experience.[29] Much (deconstructive) postmodernism, by regarding the soul or mind as numerically one through time, had blinded philosophers to our primary experiential basis for the idea of time.

The significance of these explanations of the origin of our basic categories, such as time, causality, and actuality (which combines the Kantian categories of "existence" and "substance"), would be hard to overstate, given the fact that Kant's "Copernican Revolution," which lies behind most forms of idealism, phenomenology, structuralism, and postmodernism, was based on the need to explain such categories while assuming, with Hume, the sensationist doctrine of perception.

Equally important to the distinction between Whitehead-based and Kant-based forms of postmodernism is the fact that Whitehead, by insisting on the reality of nonsensory perception, allows our apparent awareness of normative values to be accepted as genuine. Our moral and aesthetic discourse, accordingly, can be regarded as *cognitive*, capable of being true or false (or somewhere in between).

This point is fundamental to the respective strategies for overcoming modern scientism. Whereas Kantian forms of postmodernism, such as Richard Rorty's, put moral and aesthetic discourse on the same level with scientific discourse by denying that either type tells us about reality, Whiteheadian postmodernism achieves parity by showing how both types can express real, if partial, truths about the nature of things—partial truths it is the cultural role of philosophy to harmonize.

5 The Mechanistic View of Nature vs. Freedom

Whereas the sensationist view of perception led to contradictions between theory and practice with regard to realism, causation, the past, time, and norms, the mechanistic view of nature led to such a contradiction with regard to freedom. Early modernity reconciled human freedom with this view of nature by means of a Cartesian soul, different in kind from the stuff of which the body is composed. The relation of such a soul to its body could be explained, however, only by means of a Supernatural Coordinator (as René Descartes, Nicolas Malebranche, and Thomas Reid all agreed).

The late modern demise of supernaturalism, accordingly, entailed the transmutation of Cartesian dualism into a full-fledged materialism, in which the soul, mind, or self is taken to be merely a property or epiphenomenon of the body's brain, not an entity with any agency of its own. Whatever the "self" is, it has no power of *self*-determination. Freedom must be denied (or redefined to make it compatible with determinism, which amounts to the same thing). Some late modern philosophers explicitly admit that they must continue to presuppose freedom in practice while not being able to make sense of it in theory.[30] Much postmodernism has accentuated this contradiction, proclaiming the "disappearance of the (centered) self" while exhorting us to use our freedom to overcome oppressive views and practices.

6 Whitehead's Alternative: Panexperientialism

Whiteheadian postmodernism, instead of accepting materialism or anti-realism or returning to early modern dualism, rejects the mechanistic view of nature at the root of these stances. Its alternative view—again, anticipated by James[31]—is panexperientialism, according to which experience and thereby spontaneity, intrinsic value, and internal relations go all the way down to the most primitive units of nature.

Accordingly, besides calling all actual entities actual occasions, Whitehead also called them "occasions of experience." On the basis of panexperientialism, the unanswerable questions faced by materialists as well as dualists— *Where* and *how* did things with experience, spontaneity, intrinsic value, and internal relations emerge out of bits of matter wholly devoid of these? — need not be asked. Evolution involves real emergence, but it is the emergence of higher types of spontaneous experience out of lower types.

All such doctrines, usually under the name "panpsychism," are widely rejected as patently absurd. Such rejections often rest on characterizations that do not apply to Whiteheadian-Hartshornean panexperientialism. Critics rightly say, for example, that it would be absurd to attribute any freedom and thereby any experience to sticks and stones. But it is essential to this doctrine, the more complete name of which is "panexperientialism with organizational duality,"[32] to distinguish between aggregational organizations, which as such have no experience or spontaneity, and "compound individuals," which do.[33]

Even after becoming aware of this distinction, however, modern thinkers tend to consider panexperientialism to be self-evidently false. The same is true of the Jamesian-Whiteheadian endorsement of nonsensory perception, as evidenced by the fact that most admiring treatments of James's thought virtually ignore the fact that he endorsed the reality of telepathy and devoted much of his time to psychical research.[34]

In any case, these distinctively postmodern views about being and perceiving, besides solving various philosophical problems, also provide the basis for a distinctive type of postmodernism.

7 Comparison with the Dominant
Image of Postmodernism

The term "postmodernism" is commonly associated with a wide variety
of ideas that together constitute what can be called the "dominant
image of postmodernism." Whiteheadian postmodernism exemplifies
this dominant image in many respects.

- It rejects foundationalism and with it the quest for certainty.

- It accepts the need to deconstruct a wide range of received ideas,
  including the ontotheological idea of God, the substantial self,
  and history as having a predetermined end.

- It seeks to foster pluralism and diversity, both human and
  ecological.

But the reconstructive type of postmodernism also differs from
the dominant image of postmodernism in many respects. Some
of these differences are implicit in the very fact that this approach
is metaphysical. For example, whereas most postmodernists have
spoken derisively of the "correspondence theory of truth" and the
idea of language as "referential," reconstructive postmodernists
defend these notions, partly by pointing out that their denials lead
to what Karl-Otto Apel and Jürgen Habermas call "performative
contradictions,"[35] partly by showing how Whitehead's philosophy,
with its panexperientialist ontology and nonsensationist view of
perception, overcomes the standard objections.[36]

Closely related is the fact that reconstructive postmodernism,
while rejecting foundationalism, also rejects a complete relativism
of both truth and value.[37] Central to avoiding relativism with
regard to truth is the acceptance of the inevitable presuppositions of
practice, which some of us call "hard-core commonsense notions,"
as universally valid criteria of adequacy.[38] The avoidance of complete
relativism with regard to normative values is based partly on the fact

that the nonsensationist doctrine of perception allows for a direct (albeit not infallible) perception of such values. The idea that such norms or values somehow exist so as to be prehendable, however, requires another topic, the existence of God—a subject that brings us to distinctively theological doctrines.

8 Postmodern Christian Doctrines

Conservative-to-fundamentalist theologians have said that modern liberal theology has become increasingly vacuous. Although reconstructive postmodern theologians agree, they argue that the problem with modern liberalism was not its liberal worldview and method, according to which supernaturalism is rejected and the truth of religious beliefs is to be based on experience and reason rather than the authority of scripture and tradition. The problem, instead, was its acceptance of the modern assumptions discussed earlier. If those assumptions are accepted, so that reason is equated with *modern* reason, there is no disputing those postmodernists who believe it impossible for a theology to be both reasonable and robust.[39] By rejecting those assumptions, however, a postmodern liberal theology can develop robust Christian doctrines.

NATURALISTIC THEISM

At the heart of this theology is its naturalistic theism. As explained in Chapter 1, process theism "is naturalistic not in the sense of equating God with 'nature' or otherwise denying distinct agency to God, but simply in the sense of rejecting supernaturalism, understood as the doctrine of a divine being that can interrupt the world's normal causal principles." This rejection is rooted in its view of the relation of God to being itself, which it renames "creativity" to reflect the fact that that which all beings embody is not passive stuff but dynamic energy. Creativity, more precisely, is each actual occasion's twofold power to exercise a modicum of self-determination (final causation) and then to exert influence (efficient causation) on future events. Traditional theism, with its equation of God with being itself, said that this twofold power is essentially embodied in God alone. Because any power possessed by creatures is a gift, the normal causal patterns among creatures could be interrupted at any time. This position was fully enunciated only with the postbiblical development of the doctrine of creation *ex nihilo*. Whiteheadian postmodern theologians return to the view, common to Plato, the Bible, and most Christian thinkers prior to the end of second century A.D., that our universe was created by God's bringing a particular type of order out of chaos.[40]

DEMONIC EVIL

The necessity for this type of creation, involving a long evolutionary process, is explained in terms of the idea that creative power is essentially embodied in a world of finite actualities as well as in the divine actuality. The divine power, accordingly, is necessarily persuasive. It could not be coercive in the sense of unilaterally determining what happens in the world. This view provides the basis for a theodicy that defends the perfect goodness of our creator without minimizing the evil of our world.[41]

The distinction between God and creativity provides, in fact, the basis for a robust doctrine of demonic evil, with the basic idea being that God's creation of human beings brought into existence a level of worldly creativity that not only could become diametrically opposed to the divine creativity but could also do so with sufficient power to threaten divine purposes.[42]

This view of the God-world relation also reconciles theism with the scientific community's naturalistic assumption that no events, however extraordinary, involve violations of the world's basic causal principles.[43]

VARIABLE DIVINE INFLUENCE

The naturalism of this theism does not, however, prevent it from endorsing the assumption of Christian faith that God acts variably in the world, so that some events are "acts of God" in a special sense. The key idea here is that although divine action is formally the same in every event, it can differ radically in content, effectiveness, and, at the human level, the role it plays in the constitution of the self.

On the basis of these ideas, reconstructive postmodern theologians have entered into the traditional discussion of how God was literally incarnate in Jesus, arguing for a position that overcomes the standard dichotomy of regarding Jesus as wholly "different in kind" or merely "different in degree" from other human beings.[44] They have also argued that this type of naturalism, with its variable divine influence, can, unlike neo-Darwinism, illuminate both the directionality and apparent jumps in the evolutionary process.[45] This form of liberal theology has thereby provided far more robust doctrines of divine creation and incarnation than found in *modern* liberal theologies.

RELIGIOUS PLURALISM

This return to traditional concerns regarding divine creation and incarnation is sometimes accompanied by a return to ontological wrestling with the Christian idea of God as trinitarian.[46] Such thinking, besides providing the basis for Christological reflection, has also been employed to relate Christian faith to other religions, especially insofar as the resulting trinitarianism involves the distinction between God and creativity (or being itself). This topic is covered in Chapter 4.

The affirmation of life after death is possible for postmodern process theology, in spite of its rejection of supernaturalism and appeals to authority, because its rejection of sensationism allows it to take seriously the empirical evidence for life after death.[47] It is this feature of this type of theology that is probably most important for its intention to provide a form of liberal theology that, by being sufficiently robust to be widely acceptable in the churches, can overcome modernity's liberal-conservative antithesis.[48]

THEOLOGY AND ETHICS

Reconstructive postmodern theology wants to overcome the modern separation, opposed by the various types of liberation theology, between theology and ethics. "A postmodern theology," it declares, "must be a liberation theology," which means, among other things, that doctrines of God, sin, and salvation must be articulated with "reference to the concrete sins from which God is presumably trying to save us."[49] One of these sins is certainly modern society's treatment of the earth, which has resulted in a global ecological crisis. Partly because of its panexperientialism, according to which individuals at all levels have intrinsic value and are internally related to individuals at all other levels, Whiteheadian postmodern theology has devoted great attention to this issue from the time the human threat to the environment came into general consciousness.[50] Biologist Charles Birch's term for this perspective was, in fact, the "postmodern ecological worldview."[51] This term points to one of the most significant differences from Kant-based types of postmodernism, which, rather than overcoming the human alienation from nature fostered by modern dualism, intensify this alienation by portraying nature as simply a human construct.[52]

A closely related sin taken with utmost seriousness by postmodern process theologians is patriarchy, with Cobb suggesting: "Culturally and intellectually, the most important movement of the twentieth century may prove to have been feminism."[53] Unlike those postmodernists who see the source of our problems as having arisen about four hundred years ago, Catherine Keller pointed out that feminists date it about four *thousand* years ago, when androcentric history began in earnest. She maintained, nevertheless, that feminism is a *conditio sine qua non* of any genuinely postmodern world.[54]

As illustrated by Keller's writings and those of Carol Christ,[55] there are many features of this type of postmodern theology—including its rejection of divine power as unilateral determination, its emphasis on divine responsiveness, and its emphasis on internal relations, all of which cut against portraying the divine and the human in stereotypically masculine terms—that provide ontological support for cultural feminism, especially ecofeminism.

Closely related to this theology's support for both ecological and feminist liberation is its dedication to liberating the planet from modern economism, with its ideology of unending economic growth. Far from promoting the common good, this ideology, which has replaced nationalism as the global religion,[56] has undermined communities, destroyed the environment, and increased the gap between rich and poor.[57] Indeed, argues Cobb, it is through modern political and economic theory that modern thought, with its dualism and individualism, has had its most significant and harmful influence on our present situation.[58] A postmodern economic theory would be based on the (Whiteheadian) idea of "persons-in-community," with the community to which we are internally related being at least the entire living world.[59]

This theology also seeks liberation from the global political order distinctive of modernity. One feature of this order that has been opposed is its militarism, which now includes nuclearism.[60] But the more general feature of the modern world order is the system of sovereign states, rooted in the Peace of Westphalia of 1648 and early modern political theorists such as Hugo Grotius and Thomas Hobbes. This international anarchy not only provides the permitting cause of militarism, it is argued, but also prevents solutions to four other problems equally interlocked with the global economy: the global ecological crisis, global apartheid, massive human rights abuses, and the undermining of national and local democracies.[61]

Replacing this order with a postmodern world would require the creation of democracy at the global level. The Christian rationale for global democracy is that it is a necessary condition for a world ruled by divine rather than demonic values, for which Christians pray every time we repeat the Lord's prayer.[62]

Notes

1 A. N. Whitehead, *Science and the Modern World* (The Free Press, 1967), 143.

2 John B. Cobb, Jr., "From Crisis Theology to the Post-Modern World," *Centennial Review* 8 (Spring 1964), 209–20; reprinted in Thomas J. J. Altizer, ed., *Toward a New Christianity: Readings in the Death of God Theology* (Harcourt, Brace and World, 1967) and several other anthologies.

3 Cobb, *God and the World* (Westminster Press, 1967), 135, 138; "The Possibility of Theism Today," in Edward H. Madden et al. eds., *The Idea of God: Philosophical Perspectives* (Charles C. Thomas, 1968), 98–123, at 105.

4 Griffin, "Post-Modern Theology for a New Christian Experience," in David Ray Griffin and Thomas J. J. Altizer, eds., *John Cobb's Theology in Process* (Westminster Press, 1977), 5–24.

5 Cobb, *Christ in a Pluralistic Age* (Westminster Press, 1975), 15, 25–27.

6 Floyd W. Matson, *The Broken Image: Man, Science and Society* (1964; Doubleday, 1966), vi, 139, 228.

7 Harold K. Schilling, *The New Consciousness in Science and Religion* (United Church Press, 1973), 44–47, 73–74, 191, 183, 244–53.

8 Charles Altieri, "From Symbolist Thought to Immanence: The Ground of Postmodern American Poetics," *Boundary* 2:1 (1973), 605–42.

9 Frederick Ferré, *Shaping the Future: Resources for the Post-Modern World* (Harper & Row, 1976), 100, 106–7.

10 John Hick, ed., *The Myth of God Incarnate* (SCM Press, 1977).

11 Griffin, "Myth, Incarnation, and the Need for a Postmodern Theology," unpublished MS (available at the Center for Process Studies), 34.

12 *The Reenchantment of Science: Postmodern Proposals* and *Spirituality and Society: Postmodern Visions,* both of which I edited, and *God and Religion in the Postmodern World,* which contains my own essays (all published in 1988 by the State University of New York Press).

13 John Herman Randall, Jr., "The Nature of Naturalism," Yervant

H. Krikorian, ed., *Naturalism and the Human Spirit* (Columbia University Press, 1944), esp. 367–69.

14 Whitehead, *Science and the Modern World,* vii, 156, 185; *Process and Reality: an Essay in Cosmology,* corrected edition, ed. by David Ray Griffin and Donald W. Sherburne (The Free Press, 1978), 15.

15 Paul A. Bové, *Early Postmodernism: Foundational Essays* (Duke University, 1995).

16 Whitehead, *Process and Reality,* 3, 4.

17 Whitehead, *Modes of Thought* (The Free Press, 1968), 3.

18 *Science and the Modern World,* vii, 187; *Adventures of Ideas* (The Free Press, 1967), 226.

19 *Modes of Thought,* 116.

20 *Process and Reality,* 8, 9, xiv.

21 Whitehead, *The Function of Reason* (Boston: Beacon Press, 1958), 49.

22 *Process and Reality,* 15.

23 Cobb, "Introduction" to *Postmodernism and Public Policy: Reframing Religion, Culture, Education, Sexuality, Class, Race, Politics, and the Economy* (State University of New York Press, 2002).

24 William A. Beardslee, "Christ in the Postmodern Age: Reflections inspired by Jean-Francois Lyotard," in David Ray Griffin, William A. Beardslee, and Joe Holland, eds., *Varieties of Postmodern Theology* (State University of New York Press, 1989), 63–80; "Stories in the Postmodern World: Orienting and Disorienting," in Griffin, ed., *Sacred Interconnections: Postmodern Spirituality, Political Economy, and Art* (State University of New York Press, 1990), 163–76.

25 *Process and Reality,* 153.

26 Ibid., 13.

27 George Santayana, *Skepticism and Animal Faith* (Dover, 1955), 14–15.

28 *Symbolism: Its Meaning and Effect* (1927; G. P. Putnam's Sons, 1959).

29 Whitehead, *Adventures of Ideas,* 220–21.

30 John Searle, *Minds, Brains, and Science* (British Broadcasting Corporation, 1984), 85–86, 92–98.

31   Marcus P. Ford, *William James's Philosophy: a New Perspective* (University of Massachusetts Press, 1982); "William James," in David Ray Griffin, John B. Cobb, Jr., Marcus P. Ford, and Pete A. Y. Gunter, *Founders of Constructive Postmodern Philosophy: Peirce, James, Bergson, Whitehead, and Hartshorne* (State University of New York Press, 1993), 89–132.

32   Griffin, "Introduction" to *Reenchantment without Supernaturalism: a Process Philosophy of Religion* (Cornell University Press, 2001).

33   Griffin, *Unsnarling the World-Knot: Consciousness, Freedom, and the Mind-Body Problem* (University of California Press, 1998), chs. 7, 9.

34   Marcus Ford, "William James"; "James's Psychical Research and Its Philosophical Implications," *Transactions of the Charles S. Peirce Society* 34 (1998), 605–26.

35   Martin Jay, "The Debate over Performative Contradiction: Habermas versus the Poststructuralists," Jay, *Force Fields: Between Intellectual History and Cultural Critique* (Routledge, 1993), 25–37.

36   Cobb, "Alfred North Whitehead," in Griffin et al., *Founders of Constructive Postmodern Philosophy*, 165–95, esp. 181–87; Griffin, *Reenchantment without Supernaturalism*, Ch. 9.

37   Cobb, *Postmodernism and Public Policy*, Ch. 2.

38   Griffin, "Introduction," *Founders*, 1–42, esp. 23–29; *Unsnarling*, Ch. 2, "Confusion about Common Sense."

39   Jeffrey Stout, *The Flight from Authority: Religion, Morality, and the Quest for Autonomy* (University of Notre Dame Press, 1981), 118, 140, 146; *Adventures of Ideas*, 220-21.

40   Griffin, "Creation out of Nothing, Creation out of Chaos, and the Problem of Evil," in Stephen T. Davis, ed., *Encountering Evil*, 2nd ed. (Westminster/John Knox, 2001); Catherine Keller, *The Face of the Deep: A Theology of Becoming* (Routledge, 2003).

41   Griffin, "Creation out of Nothing"; *God, Power, and Evil: a Process Theodicy* (Westminster, 1976); *Evil Revisited: Responses and Reconsiderations* (State University of New York Press, 1991).

42   Marjorie Suchocki, *The Fall to Violence: Original Sin in Relational Theology* (Continuum, 1994); Griffin, *Evil Revisited*, 31–33; "Why Demonic Power Exists: Understanding the Church's Enemy" and

"Overcoming the Demonic: the Church's Mission," *Lexington Theological Review* 28 (1993), 223–60.

43 Griffin, *Religion and Scientific Naturalism: Overcoming the Conflicts* (State University of New York Press, 2000).

44 Cobb, *Christ in a Pluralistic Age*, chs. 7–10; *Postmodernism and Public Policy*, Ch. 1.

45 Griffin, *Religion and Scientific Naturalism*, Ch. 8.

46 Joseph A. Bracken, S. J., and Marjorie Hewitt Suchocki, ed., *Trinity in Process: a Relational Theology of God* (Continuum, 1997).

47 Cobb, "The Resurrection of the Soul," *Harvard Theological Review* 80 (1987), 213–27; Griffin, *God and Religion*, Ch. 6; *Evil Revisited*, 34–40; *Reenchantment without Supernaturalism*, Ch. 6.

48 Cobb, *Christ in a Pluralistic Age*, 15, 27; Griffin, *God and Religion*, 2, 6; "Liberal but not Modern: Overcoming the Liberal-Conservative Antithesis," *Lexington Theological Review* 28 (1993), 201–22.

49 Griffin, "Postmodern Theology as Liberation Theology: A Response to Harvey Cox," Griffin, Beardslee, and Holland, *Varieties of Postmodern Theology*, 81–94, at 81.

50 Cobb, *Is it Too Late? A Theology of Ecology* (Bruce, 1972); Griffin, "Whitehead's Contributions to a Theology of Nature," *Bucknell Review* 20 (1972), 3–24; Charles Birch and Cobb, *The Liberation of Life: from the Cell to the Community* (Cambridge University Press, 1981); Birch, *Confronting the Future* (1976; rev. ed., Penguin Books, 1993); *Regaining Compassion for Humanity and Nature* (New South Wales University Press, 1993); Jay B. McDaniel, *Of God and Pelicans: a Theology for the Reverence of Life* (Westminster/John Knox, 1989).

51 Birch, *On Purpose* (New South Wales University Press, 1990), xvi, 73–85, 114–37

52 Cobb, *Postmodernism and Public Policy*, Ch. 5.

53 Ibid., Ch. 4.

54 Keller, "Toward a Postpatriarchal Postmodernity," in Griffin, ed., *Spirituality and Society*, 63–80, at 64, 74.

55 Carol P. Christ, *Rebirth of the Goddess: Finding Meaning in Feminist Spirituality* (Addison-Wesley, 1997), 104–7.

56   John B. Cobb, Jr., *The Earthist Challenge to Economism: A Theological Critique of the World Bank* (Macmillan, 1999), 13–27.

57   Herman E. Daly, "The Steady-State Economy: Postmodern Alternative to Growthmania," in Griffin, ed., *Spirituality and Society*, 107–22; Daly and Cobb, *For the Common Good: Redirecting the Economy Toward Community, the Environment, and a Sustainable Future*, 2nd ed. (Beacon Press, 1994).

58   Cobb, *Postmodernism and Public Policy*, Ch. 5.

59   Cobb, "From Individualism to Persons in Community: a Postmodern Economic Theory," Griffin, ed., *Sacred Interconnections*, 123–42; *Postmodernism and Public Policy*, Ch. 3; Daly and Cobb, *For the Common Good*, Ch. 8

60   Keller, "Warriors, Women, and the Nuclear Complex: Toward a Postnuclear Postmodernity," *Sacred Interconnections*, 63–82; Griffin, "Peace and the Postmodern Paradigm," *Spirituality and Society*, 143–54; "Imperialism, Nuclearism, and Postmodern Theism," *God and Religion*, 127–45.

61   Chapter 6, "Divine Goodness and Demonic Evil."

62   Chapter 4, "Process Eschatology."

CHAPTER THREE

Theism and the Crisis in Moral Theory

M ODERN MORAL THEORY IS IN CRISIS. The only real solution to this crisis, a number of thinkers have argued from a variety of perspectives, is to reject the late modern conviction that ethics, meaning moral theory, must be autonomous in relation to religious beliefs, especially any type of theism. In this chapter, I advocate one version of this thesis.

1 The Modern Commitment and Autonomous Ethics

Most premodern and early modern moral theory was theistic. Although different schools of thought had different ideas about various details, most thinkers agreed that morality was divinely sanctioned, so that ethics—that is, moral theory—would be, in the phrase John Mackie made famous, "part of the fabric of the world." Insofar as this theistic framework was taken for granted, all sorts of questions typical of recent ethical reflection—whether moral statements can be true, whether they are even cognitively meaningful, whether philosophers can provide justification and motivation for the moral life—did not arise.

For various reasons, nevertheless, much Enlightenment thought decided that ethics needed to become autonomous, weaning itself from all dependence on theistic presuppositions. Although various considerations fed into this conclusion, a crucial one—famously stated in Kant's dictum that "enlightenment" means thinking for oneself—was the insistence that human thought is to break free of all authority. Franklin Gamwell, calling the insistence on autonomy in this formal sense "the modern commitment," said that "modernity is distinguished by the increasing affirmation that our understandings of reality and ourselves in relation to it cannot be validated or redeemed by appeals to some authoritative expression or tradition or institution" but "only by appeal in some sense to human experience and reason as such."[1]

This modern commitment did not by itself dictate that ethics had to become autonomous from theism. It declared only that moral thought had to be autonomous in the purely formal sense of basing its conclusions on experience and reason. There were many Enlightenment thinkers, including Francis Hutcheson, Adam Ferguson, and Thomas Jefferson, who believed that this modern approach, with its rejection of heteronomy, supported a view of divine existence that in turn supported morality.

The idea that the autonomy of thought from authority entailed the autonomy of ethics from theism followed only when it was concluded, by thinkers such as Hume and Kant, that theism—including the "deism" of thinkers such as Hutcheson, Ferguson, and Jefferson—could not be justified in terms of experience and reason alone. It was the spread of this conviction—which entailed that, in Gamwell's words, "theistic claims are, at least by implication, incurably authoritarian in character"—that provided the link between the autonomy of thought in the purely formal sense and the late modern consensus that moral claims must be justified independently of theistic affirmations.[2]

The demand for independence was not unique to ethics. The dominant consensus with regard to ethics is simply one aspect of late modern thought's consensus that *all* areas of thought must and can be worked out independently of any theistic beliefs. Charles Larmore, for example, said that "modernity requires [a] purely naturalistic explanation of nature as well as a purely human understanding of morality." Besides holding that these nontheistic explanations are *required* by modernity, Larmore also endorsed the conviction that such explanations can be *adequate*, saying: "We no longer need God to explain the world and to ground the rules of our common life."[3]

After two centuries of the attempt to develop an autonomous moral theory, however, this tradition is in crisis. For a moral theory to succeed, it must provide at least two things: (1) a credible defense of moral objectivity, meaning that some basic moral principles, such as "we should not inflict pain on others simply for fun," are objectively true; and (2) some motivation to adopt a moral way of life. But modern moral theory has failed on both counts, and this twofold failure is intimately connected with its eschewal of a theistic basis. I will illustrate this claim first with regard to moral objectivity.

2 The Failure to Provide Moral Objectivity

In light of Western thought's traditional way of explaining the objectivity of moral principles, the failure of late modern thought is no cause for surprise. This objectivity was based on *moral realism*, according to which normative moral values exist in the nature of things. Because this view was formulated paradigmatically by Plato, as part of his more general affirmation of the existence of ideal forms, it is often called "Platonic realism." This affirmation raised, however, what can be called "the Platonic problem"—namely, the question of *how* and *where* such forms could exist.

Plato himself seemed to imply that the ideal forms somehow existed on their own ("in the void," as it were), a view that Aristotle and other critics found unintelligible, holding instead that abstract, ideal entities can exist only in concrete, actual entities. Middle

Platonism solved this problem with the doctrine that the forms exist in "the mind of God," a thesis that was adopted in most medieval philosophy.

This doctrine also solved, in advance, what can be called "the Benacerraf problem." Paul Benacerraf argued (rightly) that true beliefs can be considered *knowledge* only if that which makes the belief true is somehow *causally* responsible for the belief.[4] For example, my true beliefs about a tree in my garden can be considered knowledge only if the tree's causation is partly responsible for my beliefs.

Although Benacerraf was focusing on the question of mathematical knowledge, his argument applies also moral knowledge. Moral beliefs cannot be considered knowledge unless, besides being true, they are somehow causally derivative from whatever it is—such as a set of normative values inherent in the fabric of the universe—that makes the beliefs true. The Benacerraf problem is how normative values, being merely ideal entities, could exert causal efficacy, thereby bringing about true moral beliefs. The doctrine that normative moral forms are in God provided the answer that these ideal entities are given causal efficacy by divine agency.

The decision that moral theory must be autonomous from all forms of theism, however, meant that the Platonic and Benacerraf problems had lost their long-standing answer. Part of the recent crisis in ethics is due to the resulting loss of faith in moral realism, as can be illustrated by the positions of John Mackie and Gilbert Harman.

Mackie, in his well-known book *Ethics*, announced his rejection of moral realism with his subtitle, *Inventing Right and Wrong*, along with his denial that values are "part of the fabric of the world."[5] Referring to the idea that "if someone is writhing in agony before your eyes" you should "do something about it if you can," Mackie said that such claims are *not* "objective, intrinsic, requirements of the nature of things."[6] In explaining the basis for this denial, he said: "The difficulty of seeing how values could be objective is a fairly strong reason for thinking that they are not."[7]

The difficulty in question involved what Mackie called "the argument from queerness," the metaphysical dimension of it in particular. (The argument also includes an epistemological dimension, mentioned below.) Objective values "would be entities or qualities or relations of a very strange sort, utterly different from anything else in the universe" because they would have *prescriptivity* built into them, as do some Platonic Forms. The Form of the Good, for example, "has to-be-pursuedness somehow built into it."[8]

Mackie fully admitted that his view, according to which "[t]here are no objective values,"[9] does not do justice to ordinary moral thought, because "most people in making moral judgments implicitly claim, among other things, to be pointing to something objectively prescriptive"—a claim Mackie had to consider simply false.[10] Mackie also admitted that his argument from queerness depended upon the presumption of atheism.

Describing his book as "a discussion of what we can make of morality without recourse to God," he added: "I concede that if the requisite theological doctrine could be defended, a kind of objective ethical prescriptivity could be defended."[11] Mackie rejected moral realism on the basis of what seems to be an implicit appeal to the Platonic problem — where could values exist? — and the Benacerraf problem — how could abstract forms have prescriptivity built into them?

Harman, suggesting that he will do more justice to ordinary moral thinking than did Mackie, said that "if a philosophical theory conflicts with ordinary ways of thinking and speaking, . . . something has probably gone wrong."[12] Indeed, having defined nihilism as "the doctrine that there are no moral facts, no moral truths, and no moral knowledge," Harman says early in his book that he will retain "our ordinary views and [avoid] endorsing some form of nihilism."[13]

By the end of the book, however, we learn that "there are no absolute facts of right or wrong, apart from one or another set of conventions," but only "relative facts about what is right or wrong"—relative, that is, to some set of conventions adopted by a particular society,[14] which is exactly the nihilistic position. Accordingly, in spite of Harman's statement that something has probably gone wrong "if a philosophical theory conflicts with ordinary ways of thinking and speaking," he says: "We cannot have morality as it is ordinarily conceived."[15]

This conclusion depends partly on the Platonic problem. If we approach moral theory from a scientific viewpoint, Harman said, we should "concentrate on finding the place of value and obligation in the world of facts as revealed by science." His conclusion with regard to objective values, however, is that "our scientific conception of the world has no place for entities of this sort"[16]—a conclusion that follows from Harman's assertion that science entails naturalism, defined as "the sensible thesis that *all* facts are facts of nature."[17] Naturalism, thus defined, rules out the existence of a divine actuality: "Our scientific conception of the world has no place for gods."[18] The implication is that because "nature" neither includes, nor is included in, nor is the product of, a divine being, there is no "place" for normative values.

Harman's conclusion that ordinary morality, with its belief in objective values, cannot be supported is also based partly on the Benacerraf problem. At the heart of Harman's argument against the idea that moral belief can constitute knowledge is his claim that whereas scientific assertions are based on observations of facts, moral assertions are *not*.

His basis for this distinction is that, whereas we can perceive physical facts through our physical senses, "there does not seem to be any way in which the actual rightness or wrongness of a given situation can have any effect on your perceptual apparatus."[19] Although this claim is partly based, like the epistemological dimension of Mackie's queerness argument,[20] on the sensationist doctrine of perception, Harman also referred to Benacerraf's essay.

The views of Mackie and Harman are representative of many moral philosophers. In a symposium on Mackie's moral thought, for example, R. M. Hare said, nonchalantly: "It was John Mackie's great contribution to ethics to display clearly the absurdity of realism."[21] Late modern moral philosophy is in crisis partly because this view is widespread. Another reason, however, is that it cannot provide motivation to be moral.

3 The Failure to Provide Motivation to be Moral

In light of the basis for motivation provided by traditional thought, it should be no surprise that late modern moral theory, with its autonomy from religious belief, has also failed in this respect. That traditional basis was what Clifford Geertz calls the "religious perspective," which involves "the conviction that the values one holds are grounded in the inherent structure of reality, that between the way one ought to live and the way things really are there is an unbreakable inner connection."[22] This feature of the religious perspective accounts for religion's moral vitality: "The powerfully coercive 'ought' is felt to grow out of a comprehensive factual 'is' . . . [The power of sacred symbols] comes from their presumed ability to identify fact with value at the most fundamental level."[23]

Geertz's characterization of a "comprehensive factual 'is,'" in which "fact and value [are identified] at the most fundamental level," is a characterization of the Holy — of something that is intrinsically good in an ultimate, nonderivative sense. In traditional cultures, the ultimate motivation for the moral life could be provided by some such idea because the Holy Reality is a fact — an "is" — that generates a powerful "ought."

The way in which a moral "ought" is uniquely generated from a Holy "is" can be called "the logic of the holy." This logical argument, usually only implicit, can be explicated thus:

1. The Holy Reality wants us to X.

2. We want to be in harmony with the Holy Reality (because it is that which is good in an ultimate, nonderivative way).

3. To be in harmony with the Holy Reality requires that
    we X.

4. Therefore we ought to X.

When Hume famously argued that an "ought" cannot be
deduced from an "is," he failed to reflect on the exceptional nature
of a *holy* "is." However, given the correctness of his observation, this
important exception aside, it would seem likely that ethics, once
disconnected from any belief in a Holy Reality, would be unable to
provide justification and motivation for a moral life. This is indeed
what we find.

Bernard Williams wrote a book with the title *Ethics and the
Limits of Philosophy*, by which he meant that morality "can[not] be
justified by philosophy."[24] Although Williams made some of the same
points as Mackie and Harman, he focused on the issue of motivation.
Indicating that the crucial event in this regard was the collapse of
teleological assumptions, he added: "No one has yet found a good way
of doing without those assumptions."[25] The loss of those assumptions
led to the discovery (as Williams called it) that "our values are not 'in
the world,'" with this being the basic idea behind the realization (as
Williams regarded it) that it is a fallacy—the *naturalistic* fallacy—to
think that value could somehow be derived from fact, so that *ought*
could be derived from *is*.[26]

Because the loss of teleology was part and parcel of the decline
of theism, it was this decline that Williams saw as the crucial event
behind the loss of moral realism. Williams made this connection
explicitly in commenting on the question "what it could mean to say
that a requirement or demand was 'part of the fabric of the world.'"
It "might possibly mean," Williams pointed out, "that some agency
which made the demand or imposed the requirement was part of the
fabric."[27] It was because Williams did not believe in such an agency
that he rejected moral realism and thereby the possibility of justify-
ing morality. Accordingly, Williams could have titled his book, more
modestly, *Ethics and the Limits of Atheistic Philosophy*.

The centrality of Williams' presumption of atheism to his argument is revealed in his answer to this question: What does it mean that we have an inescapable sense that some things are important, not merely for some people, but "important uberhaupt"? His response: "It does not mean that it is important to the universe; in that sense, nothing is important."[28]

To *affirm* that something is important to the universe is a way of expressing the theistic idea that the universe itself has a perspective—indeed, the ultimate perspective—on things. To *deny* this is a way of denying that there is anything holy—any comprehensive "is" from which an "ought" could be generated. Given this denial, Williams saw no way in which philosophy can say anything that could motivate people to take the moral, meaning the impartial, point of view.

Williams' critique on this point was especially directed at Kantians, who believe that the moral point of view can be justified without moral realism, out of reason alone. "[T]here is no route to the impartial standpoint from rational deliberation alone," Williams argued, because:

> The *I* that stands back in rational reflection from my desires
> is still the *I* that has those desires and will, empirically and
> concretely, act; and it is not, simply by standing in reflection,
> converted into a being whose fundamental interest lies in the
> harmony of all interests. It cannot, just by taking this step,
> acquire the motivations of justice.[19]

Such motivations could be provided, the message of Williams' book is, only by a view of our place in the universe that, with the decline of theistically rooted teleology, is no longer possible.

Jürgen Habermas was a Kantian philosopher who would at first glance seem to differ with Williams. Emphasizing the nontheistic context of contemporary ethical philosophy, Habermas said that we need "a posttraditional" or "postmetaphysical" morality, meaning one that has "detached itself from the religious and metaphysical context from which it arose."[30] Such a position, he claimed, "can explicate the moral point of view," which means the impartial point of view.[31]

Habermas might thereby seem to be claiming to do what Williams said cannot be done. But Habermas conceded that because his position cannot say that in our moral life "something incomparably important is involved"—because one cannot "salvage an unconditional meaning without God"—his position cannot "provide a motivating response to the question of . . . why we should be moral at all."[32]

For motivation, Habermas says, we must rely on socialization, especially from religion.[33] Although Habermas emphasizes what autonomous reason *can* do while Williams emphasizes what it *cannot*, they both agree that because it cannot speak of something incomparably important—of something holy—it cannot provide motivation to take the moral point of view.

4 A Growing Consensus

On the basis of the above and similar writings, a consensus has been growing that autonomous moral theory has failed. Alasdair MacIntyre, referring to the modern idea of "rights attaching to human beings simply *qua* human beings," contended that "there are no such rights, and belief in them is one with belief in witches and unicorns." The best reason for asserting that there are no rights, continued MacIntyre, is "of precisely the same type as the best reason which we possess for asserting that there are no witches and . . . no unicorns: every attempt to give good reasons for believing that there *are* such rights has failed."[34] By "every attempt," MacIntyre meant every attempt within what he calls "the Enlightenment project" of providing "a secular, rational justification for [one's] moral allegiances"[35]—the project of autonomous ethics.

In an essay entitled "God or Mackie? The Dilemma of Secular Moral Philosophy," J. D. Goldsworthy, after reviewing the work of various Kantian theorists as well as Mackie and MacIntyre, said that "moral philosophers have conspicuously failed to find any plausible foundation for the supposed authority of moral precepts." "It seems doubtful," Goldsworthy added, "that any secular philosophy can carry ethics to higher ground."[36]

Jeffrie Murphy, reflecting on the fact that recent moral and legal philosophers have found it difficult to provide a basis for affirming universal human rights, wrote:

> [W]e at present live in a time when it is widely believed—under the impact of work by such writers in the 'analytic' tradition as Gilbert Harman and John Mackie and such writers in the 'pluralist' tradition as Richard Rorty and Alasdair MacIntyre—that all . . . attempts rationally to demonstrate the objective corrrectness of certain moral claims are doomed to failure.[37]

Murphy especially found it disturbing that such philosophers could not explain "why anyone is morally required to *care* whether or not another's situation is worsened."[38] Murphy connected this failure with the divorce of ethics from theism, a fact that is especially significant in light of the fact that he had previously argued that morality does not depend on belief in God, so that Nietzsche's proclamation that "God is dead" was no "big deal."[39] Now, however, having realized that the idea of human rights presupposes the notion that human beings are somehow sacred, Murphy asked, rhetorically: "How can one expect to dump God and a religious vision of the universe and yet retain a strong concept of the *sacredness* of anything?"[40]

Basil Mitchell, in *Morality: Religious and Secular: The Dilemma of the Traditional Conscience*, likewise argued that secular ethics has failed. By the "traditional conscience," Mitchell referred to people who, while giving up the religious basis for morality and hence the idea that morality "was based on a purpose written in the nature of things," still hold that we should obey our traditional moral intuitions.[41] The "dilemma" for such people is that, given the fact that the various forms of secular humanism have failed "to provide a rationale for morality as traditionally conceived," they must either modify their conscience or question their secular assumptions.[42] Mitchell's book is an argument for the second option and hence for a return to religious morality, grounded in theism.

5 Is a Return to Theistic Ethics Possible?

Mitchell's book is only one of many recent writings that, reflecting on the failure of secular moral theory, call for a return to theistic ethics. Most of these writings, however, fail to address the fact that such a return is, for most thinkers who have rejected theism, simply inconceivable. The dilemma faced by those who have recognized the instability of a purely secular humanism is, therefore, even worse than Mitchell says. The dilemma is that although they recognize the need for a justification of some basic moral principles that a nonreligious ethic cannot provide, they also find themselves unable to return to the kind of religious worldview evidently required. For example, Jeffrie Murphy, having argued that "the liberal theory of rights requires a doctrine of human dignity, preciousness and sacredness that cannot be utterly detached from a belief in God or at least from a world view that could be properly called religious in some metaphysically profound sense," added:

> For those, such as I, who find it very difficult—perhaps impossible—to embrace religious convictions, the idea that fundamental moral values may require such convictions is not one to be welcomed with joy. This idea generates tensions and appears to force choices that some of us would prefer not to make.[43]

The mere fact that people see a "need" for religious belief does not settle anything, because this perceived need may be outweighed by a conviction that a religious view, especially a theistic one, is impossible. An argument for returning to theistic moral theory, to be credible, would need to include at least the following ingredients.

The argument, for starters, must recognize that the original rejection of theism was not made lightly or without many good reasons.

This rejection, which involved one of the greatest cultural upheavals in the history of Western civilization, involved much soul-searching on the part of thousands of highly intelligent and sensitive individuals. Many of these individuals realized that the effects—both religious and moral, both personal and institutional—would be catastrophic.

They concluded, nonetheless, that the received idea of God was both intellectually incredible and morally perverse—recall Stendahl's quip that God's only excuse is that He does not exist! The reasons for rejecting this idea of God were at least as persuasive as the present reasons for saying that nonreligious moral theory is inadequate. The idea of a "return to theism" cannot, therefore, be equated with a return to *traditional* theism. It must be a "return forward," to something quite different.

The argument for such a theism must show that it, besides grounding traditional moral principles at least as well as traditional theism, overcomes its many problems. One problem was the fact that, in spite of all the arguments made on its behalf, traditional theism could not really be rationally justified, so its acceptance finally rested on authority. This fact about traditional theism is widely applied to theism as such. Habermas, for example, dismissed the possibility of a theistic grounding for morality because theism cannot be "vindicated before the tribunal of justificatory discourse."[44]

A distinction crucially needed here is that between genus and species. If a genus has more than one species, it is a logical error to dismiss the genus on the basis of only one of its species. Traditional theism, held by Augustine, Thomas, Calvin, Luther, Descartes, Newton, and Paley, has certainly been the best-known species of theism in the West. But it is far from the only one. Philosophers cannot justifiably infer from its defects that similar defects would necessarily infect all other species of theism worthy of the name.

The importance of this elementary logical point can be seen by reflection on Mackie's admission that "if the requisite theological doctrine could be defended, a kind of objective ethical prescriptivity could be defended." Mackie quickly dismissed this possibility because he considered the existence of God to be highly improbable, especially in light of the problem of evil—a conclusion toward which he argued in a subsequent book, *The Miracle of Theism: Arguments for and against the Existence of God*. An examination of his argument, however, reveals that it deals only with traditional theism, according to which one of God's attributes is "able to do everything (i.e., omnipotent)."[45]

Mackie's conclusions that the world's evil renders *this* being's existence highly unlikely is accepted by most defenders of nontraditional versions of theism. Mackie himself, in fact, pointed out that his argument would cause no difficulty for forms of theism that do not accept the traditional view of divine power.[46] But Mackie did not highlight this crucial admission. As a result, his book has been widely accepted as an argument—as the title suggests—against theism as such and hence as an argument for the probable truth of atheism.

Once we clearly make the genus-species distinction between theism as such and traditional theism, however, we can see that Mackie's book says nothing about whether one of the forms of theism that he did not examine might be rationally defensible and, indeed, might seem more probable than atheism. A similar point can be made about Habermas. Although Habermas's whole program rested on the assumption that theological discourse is cognitively inadequate, he for the most part simply repeated Kant's conclusions about traditional theism.

One will look in vain in the writings of Habermas for any examination of the many varieties of theism that have arisen since the time of Kant. Insofar as Habermas, Mackie, and the other nontheistic thinkers have not even examined these other forms of theism, there is certainly no reason to take them as authorities about the rational defensibility of these other doctrines. And, insofar as we consider these philosophers' views about morality inadequate, we have every reason to examine these other forms of theism, to see if they can fill the bill.

I myself have argued for the rational defensibility of a version of the process theism suggested by Alfred North Whitehead, with my defense having both negative and positive dimensions. The negative dimension involves showing that the problems that counted against traditional theism do not count against theism of this sort. The positive dimension is more ambitious, seeking to show this form of theism to be more probable than atheism.

The enterprise of engaging in "arguments for the existence of God" has been, to put it mildly, out of favor. Arguments of this kind, it is widely assumed, can easily be shown to be worthless. But it is precisely in relation to this question that it is most important to take seriously the genus-species distinction. Almost all "arguments for the existence of God" have been offered on behalf of traditional theism's idea of God. Virtually all criticisms of the arguments, therefore, have been criticisms of arguments purporting to support the existence of God thus conceived—Kant's demonstration, for example, that the design argument does not prove the existence of a deity who created the world *ex nihilo*.

Such critiques say nothing about the persuasiveness of arguments for the kind of creator envisaged by process theism, who created our world out of chaos. I have argued, in fact, that implicit in Whitehead's system are thirteen arguments for the existence of the divine being of which he wrote. With so many considerations counting in favor of the existence of this deity and none counting against it, the truth of something like process philosophy's theism is, I argue, "overwhelmingly more probable than the truth of atheism."

At the center of the cultural transition from theism to atheism has been the assumption that this transition is supported by the natural sciences. The most effective way to argue for the need to return to a theistic worldview, therefore, would be to show that science, far from implying atheism, cannot be made intelligible apart from a theistic framework. I will illustrate this approach in terms of one of the thirteen arguments implicit in Whitehead's philosophy, the

argument from mathematical forms — then point to its similarity to
the argument from moral norms.

6 Can the Philosophy of Mathematics Be Autonomous?

The project of making all disciplines independent from theology meant
that the philosophy of mathematics had to become autonomous. But
it, like moral philosophy, cannot answer the Platonic and Benacerraf
problems, as Reuben Hersh indicated:

> An inarticulate, half-conscious Platonism is nearly universal
> among mathematicians. . . . Yet most of this Platonism is half-
> hearted, shamefaced. We don't ask, How does this immaterial
> realm relate to material reality? How does it make contact
> with flesh and blood mathematicians? We refuse to face
> this embarrassment: Ideal entities independent of human
> consciousness violate the empiricism of modern science.

Pointing to the background of this problem, Hersh continued:

> For Leibniz and Berkeley, abstractions like numbers are
> thoughts in the mind of God. . . . [But] the Mind of God [is] no
> longer heard of in academic discourse. Yet most mathematicians
> and philosophers of mathematics continue to believe in an
> independent, immaterial abstract world — a remnant of Plato's
> Heaven . . . , with all entities but the mathematical expelled.
> Platonism without God is like the grin on Lewis Carroll's
> Cheshire cat. . . . The grin remained without the cat.[48]

The situation to which Hersh refers can be illustrated in terms
of Willard Quine's "physicalism." Although many writers equate
physicalism and materialism, Quine defined physicalism as the formal
doctrine that our ontology should be settled by the discipline of
physics. One of the ideas that is indispensable to physics, Quine
pointed out, is the existence of numbers as existing independently
of us. Quine thereby felt compelled to affirm the existence of
mathematical objects. This affirmation, however, was at odds with

Quine's emphatic contention that nothing should be allowed into our ontology that cannot pass the "tribunal of sense experience."[49]

Since sensory perception is activated only by material objects, this criterion of existence should have led Quine to a completely materialistic ontology. On the basis of his "indispensability argument," however, Quine allowed an exception, with the result that his ontology was "materialism, bluntly monistic except for the abstract objects of mathematics."[50]

This exception, however, raised a serious problem (even aside from the problem of how, given Quine's tribunal of sensory experience, we can know of the existence of mathematical objects). How is it conceivable that these abstract mathematical objects, which are not located anywhere in space or time, somehow exist, in Quine's words, "over and above the physical objects"?[51]

How and *where* would they exist in an otherwise materialistic universe? This is, of course, the "Platonic problem," but Quine failed to address it. With regard to the Benacerraf problem, Quine simply "ignore[d] the problem," as Hilary Putnam put it, "as to how we can know that abstract entities exist unless we can interact with them in some way."[52]

Other philosophers have believed that the problems cannot be ignored. Penelope Maddy put the Benacerraf problem thus:

> [H]ow can entities that don't even inhabit the physical universe take part in any causal interaction whatsoever? Surely to be abstract is to be causally inert. Thus if Platonism is true, we can have no mathematical knowledge.[53]

William Lycan, admitting that his own appeal to mathematical sets "is indeed an embarrassment to physicalism, since sets et al. are nonspatiotemporal, acausal items," said that he must either naturalize them or reject set theory.[54] To reject set theory is to reject the existence of numbers.

Although this solution has been advocated by several philosophers of mathematics — as illustrated by book titles such as *Science without*

Numbers and *Mathematics without Numbers*[55]—this "nonrealist" or "formalist" solution, most commentators agree, suffers from a fatal problem: It is inadequate to the presuppositions of mathematicians themselves. As Yiannis Moschovakis said, in a representative statement,[56] this solution violates "the instinctive certainty of most everybody who has ever tried to solve a [mathematical] problem that he is thinking about 'real objects.'"[57]

The other remaining option suggested by Lycan, to "naturalize" sets by redefining them as aspects of material things, has been developed in Penelope Maddy's *Realism in Mathematics*, which seeks to develop a materialistic version of the Platonic, realistic view. We can overcome the problem of "unobservable Platonic entities," she suggested, by "bringing [mathematical] sets into the physical world" so that they are no longer "abstract" but have "spatio-temporal location."[58] This solution, however, is clearly desperate. What could it mean to say that the entire realm of mathematics is embodied in the physical world in such a way as to be observable?

Philosophers have, as this discussion illustrates, been unable to come up with an adequate alternative to the traditional view, which explained both the locus and efficacy of mathematical objects by placing them in an all-inclusive actuality. This fact suggests that science, insofar as it requires an intelligible worldview, will need to posit such an actuality. This conclusion will be stronger, of course, to the degree that it is supported by other considerations.

One of these is the fact that Quine's indispensability argument for realism about mathematical objects is paralleled by an indispensability argument for realism about moral norms. Charles Larmore has argued that we cannot do justice to human experience unless we say, with Plato, that the world also contains not only actual things but also a realm of values.[59]

This affirmation is necessary to do justice to our moral experience, which assumes—as even Mackie and Harman agreed—that moral judgments presuppose moral truths that exist independently of our preferences.[60] But the affirmation is also necessary to do justice to *any* of our normative beliefs about values, including cognitive values about "the way we ought to think."

For example, Harman's denial of a normative realm makes it self-contradictory for him to argue that naturalism *should* be accepted.[61] In other words, the normal reasons for denying the reality of objective moral values cannot be defended without self-contradiction, because the reasons for doubting that there are moral values, such as the charge that they would be metaphysically "queer," apply equally to *cognitive* values. But to deny that there are any objective cognitive values would mean that the idea that we *ought* to avoid self-contradiction is merely a preference, with no inherent authority.[61] But such a conclusion, Larmore pointed out, involves a *reductio ad absurdum.*

> Imagine thinking that even so basic a rule of reasoning as the avoidance of contradiction has no more authority than what we choose to give it. Imagine thinking that we could just as well have willed the opposite, seeking out contradictions and believing each and every one. Has anyone the slightest idea of what it would be like really to believe this?[62]

Larmore's overall point was that anti-Platonic naturalism, if carried through consistently, "would destroy the very idea of rationality." The affirmation of a normative realm, therefore, is implied by reason as such and hence by scientific reason in particular.[63]

In spite of the cogency of this argument, however, Larmore failed to develop his Platonism into an intelligible worldview. He failed even to acknowledge the Platonic problem, and his attempt to circumvent the Benacerraf problem, as he admitted, involves "great difficulties."[64] Larmore's attempt to have Platonism without God is, as Hersh says, like trying to have the grin without the cat.

Nevertheless, in forcibly pointing out that the existence of norms is implicit in all normative thinking, Larmore is an important voice, partly because he is such a solitary one. Most philosophers nowadays either deny the reality of ideal entities altogether or, as Hersh pointed out, inconsistently retain mathematical forms while rejecting the rest. Quine, for example, enforced his "tribunal of sense experience" against moral norms while letting numbers sneak by.[65]

Harman, who denied that moral judgments can be true, as we saw, on the grounds that moral facts cannot affect our perceptual apparatus, admitted, alluding to Benacerraf, that mathematics is in the same boat:

> We do not and cannot perceive numbers. . . . Relations among numbers cannot have any more of an effect on our perceptual apparatus than moral facts can.[66]

He asserted that we can speak of mathematical knowledge, nevertheless, because mathematics is based on "indirect observational evidence."[67] This is clearly special pleading, since one can make the same claim about moral principles, as Larmore showed.

The upshot of this discussion is that, late modern dogma notwithstanding, neither the philosophy of mathematics nor the philosophy of morals can be autonomous in the sense of independent from theism. This was the position to which Alfred North Whitehead—who had spent much of his professional life dealing with mathematical principles—came in the last period of his life.

7 Whitehead on God and Moral Ideals

The point behind Hersh's metaphor of the grin needing the cat was made by Whitehead in terms of what he called the "ontological principle," one formulation of which is:

> Everything must be somewhere; and here "somewhere" means "some actual entity." Accordingly the general potentiality of the universe must be somewhere. . . . The notion of "subsistence" is merely the notion of how eternal objects can be components of the primordial nature of God.[68]

Besides answering the Platonic question about the location of ideal entities, Whitehead's ontological principle also addresses the Benacerraf question of their efficacy, saying, in another formulation, that "apart from things that are actual, there is nothing—nothing either in fact or in efficacy."[69] The eternal objects can be effective because the "primordial nature of God," which Whitehead also called "the Eros of the Universe," is "the active entertainment of all ideals, with the urge to their finite realization, each in its due season."[70]

Whitehead came to this view only late in life, after he began constructing a systematic metaphysics. Given his long involvement with mathematics and logic, he was aware that a metaphysical position would need to explain how the ideal entities studied by these disciplines could exist and be effective in the world. He also became convinced that his metaphysics needed to do justice to the fact that "the impact of aesthetic, religious and moral notions is inescapable," because a central feature of human experience is "the intuition of immediate occasions as failing or succeeding in reference to the ideal relevant to them."[71]

He realized, therefore, that his metaphysics had to have room not only for "mathematical Platonic forms," which he called "eternal objects of the objective species," but also for "eternal objects of the subjective species," which include normative values.[72]

At first Whitehead thought that an "envisagement" of the eternal objects could be attributed to the "underlying eternal energy,"[73] which he later called "creativity." But he soon realized that he could not attribute any kind of activity, even "envisagement," to energy or creativity, because to do so is to violate the ontological principle's stipulation that only *actualities* can *act*.

Whitehead's resulting conviction was that "the agency whereby ideas obtain efficiency in the creative advance" is "a basic Psyche whose active grasp of ideas conditions impartially the whole process of the Universe." Whitehead's formulation of this idea was an attempt at "understanding how the Ideals in God's nature, by reason of their status in his nature, are thereby persuasive elements in the creative advance."[74] Given this conviction — that ideal entities, including moral and aesthetic ideals, can be effective in the world in general, and therefore in human experience in particular, only by virtue of being actively envisaged by an all-inclusive actuality — our experience of ideals became evidence for the existence of such an actuality.

> There are experiences of ideals — of ideals entertained, of ideals aimed at, of ideals achieved, of ideals defaced. This is the experience of the deity of the universe. . . . The universe is thus understood as including a source of ideals. The effective aspect of this source is deity as immanent in the present experience.[75]

To give an accurate account of our moral experience, therefore, a moral philosopher needs to speak of God.

Whitehead also came to hold that theistic belief on the part of ordinary persons is necessary to sustain the moral point of view, especially in light of the fact that natural sympathy, on which Hume rested morality, does not extend, as Hume recognized, much beyond a rather limited circle.[76]

Having pointed out that modern thought, from Hume to Darwin, has eroded the basis for the humanitarian ideal, he suggested that we need "a reconstructed justification" for the cultivation of respect for human beings qua human beings.[77] In his own outline of such a justification, Whitehead ended by speaking of a "bond of sympathy" that can extend to all humanity. "This bond is the growth of reverence for that power in virtue of which nature harbours ideal ends, and produces individual beings capable of conscious discrimination of such ends. This reverence is the foundation of respect for man as man."[78]

An increasing number of philosophers, as we have seen, have come to the conclusion that motivation to live in terms of the moral point of view can finally be nourished only by a religious vision. Whitehead, besides coming to this conclusion many decades ago, also suggested, and provided a rational defense for, a new religious vision that does this while overcoming the aspects of traditional theism that have rightly caused offense.[79]

Notes

1 Franklin I. Gamwell, *The Divine Good: Modern Moral Theory and the Necessity of God* (Southern Methodist University, 1996), 3–4.

2 Ibid., 8, 1.

3 Charles Larmore, *The Morals of Modernity* (Cambridge University Press, 1996), 43, 44.

4 Paul Benacerraf, "Mathematical Truth," in *Philosophy of Mathematics*, ed. Paul Benacerraf and Hilary Putnam, 2nd ed. (1973; Cambridge University Press, 1983), 402–20.

5 John Mackie, *Ethics: Inventing Right and Wrong* (Penguin, 1977), 24.

6 Ibid., 79–80.

7 Ibid., 24.

8 Ibid., 38, 40.

9 Ibid., 15.

10 Ibid., 35, 299n.

11 Ibid., 48.

12 Gilbert Harman, *The Nature of Morality: An Introduction to Ethics* (Oxford University Press, 1977), 34.

13 Ibid., 11–13.

14 Ibid., 131–32.

15 Ibid., 90.

16 Gilbert Harman, "Is There a Single True Morality?" *Relativism: Interpretation and Confrontation*, ed. Michael Krausz (University of Notre Dame Press, 1989), 363–86, at 365, 366.

17 Ibid., 366; Harman, *The Nature of Morality*, 17.

18 Harman, "Is There a Single True Morality," 381.

19 Harman, *The Nature of Morality*, 8.

20 Mackie, *Ethics*, 38–39.

21 R. M. Hare, "Ontology in Ethics," in *Morality and Objectivity: A Tribute to J. L. Mackie*, ed. Ted Honderich (Routledge & Kegan Paul, 1985), 39–53, at 53, 42.

22 Clifford Geertz, *Islam Observed: Religious Development in Morocco and Indonesia* (Yale University Press, 1968), 97.

23 Clifford Geertz, *Interpretation of Cultures: Selected Essays* (Basic Books, 1973), 126–27.

24 Bernard Williams, *Ethics and the Limits of Philosophy* (Harvard University Press, 1985), 22.

25 Ibid., 53.

26 Ibid., 128–29.

27 Bernard Williams, "Ethics and the Fabric of the World," in *Morality and Objectivity: A Tribute to J. L. Mackie*, ed. Ted Honderich (Routledge & Kegan Paul, 1985), 203–14.

28 Williams, *Ethics and the Limits of Philosophy*, 182.

29 Ibid., 70, 69.

30 Jürgen Habermas, *Justification and Application: Remarks on Discourse Ethics*, trans. Ciaran Cronin (Polity Press, 1993), 39.

31 Ibid., 146.

32 Ibid., 71, 146.

33 Ibid., 79; Jürgen Habermas, *Postmetaphysical Thinking: Philosophical Essays*, trans. William Mark Hohengarten (MIT Press, 1992), 51; Jürgen Habermas, "Transcendence from Within, Transcendence in this World," in *Habermas, Modernity, and Public Theology*, ed. Don Browning and Francis Schüssler Fiorenza (Crossroad, 1992, 226–50, at 239.

34 Alasdair MacIntyre, *After Virtue: A Study in Moral Theory* (University of Notre Dame, 1981), 67.

35 Ibid., 65. This project, incidentally, should not be called simply the "Enlightenment project": As mentioned earlier, it was not accepted by some of the Enlightenment's leading moralists, such as Ferguson

and Hutcheson.

36 J. D. Goldsworthy, "God or Mackie? The Dilemma of Secular Moral Philosophy," *American Journal of Jurisprudence* 30 (1985): 43–78, at 45, 76.

37 Jeffrie G. Murphy, *Evolution, Morality, and the Meaning of Life* (Rowman and Littlefield, 1982), 241.

38 Ibid., 247.

39 Ibid., 16.

40 Jeffrie G. Murphy, "Constitutionalism, Moral Skepticism, and Religious Belief," in *Constitutionalism: The Philosophical Dimension*, ed. Alan S. Rosenbaum (Greenwood, 1988), 239–49, at 244.

41 Basil Mitchell, *Morality: Religious and Secular: The Dilemma of the Traditional Conscience* (Oxford University Press, 1979), 90.

42 Ibid., 91, 92.

43 Murphy, "Constitutionalism, Moral Skepticism, and Religious Belief," 248.

44 Habermas, *Justification and Application*, 146.

45 *The Miracle of Theism: Arguments for and against the Existence of God* (Clarendon, 1982), 1.

46 Ibid., 151.

47 David Ray Griffin *Reenchantment without Supernaturalism: A Process Philosophy of Religion* (Cornell University Press, 2001), 203.

48 Reuben Hersh, *What is Mathematics, Really?* (Oxford University Press, 1997), 12.

49 Willard Van Quine, *From A Logical Point of View* (Harvard University Press, 1953), 41.

50 Willard Van Quine, *From Stimulus to Science* (Harvard University Press, 1995), 14.

51 Willard Van Quine, *Theories and Things* (Harvard University Press, 1981), 14-15.

52 Hilary Putnam, *Words and Life*, ed. James Conant (Harvard University Press, 1994), 153.

53 Penelope Maddy, *Realism in Mathematics* (Clarendon Press, 1990), 37.

54 William G. Lycan, *Consciousness* (MIT Press, 1987), 90.

55 Hartry Field, *Science without Numbers* (Princeton University Press, 1980); Geoffrey, Hellman, *Mathematics without Numbers* (Oxford: Oxford University Press, 1989).

56 For similar statements from a number of other philosophers and mathematicians, see Maddy, *Realism in Mathematics*, 2–3, and Hersh, *What is Mathematics, Really?* 7.

57 Yiannis N. Moschovakis, *Descriptive Set Theory* (North Holland, 1980), 605-06. What is violated here is what mathematicians presuppose when they are actually engaged with problems. As Moschovakis pointed out, "most mathematicians claim to be formalists (when pressed)," because of the embarrassment created by the Platonic and Benacerraf problems, "while they spend their working hours behaving as if they were unabashed realists" (605–06).

58 Maddy, *Realism in Mathematics*, 44, 59, 78.

59 Larmore, *The Morals of Modernity*, 8, 86–89.

60 Ibid., 91–96.

61 Ibid., 86, 89, 114.

62 Ibid., 87, 99.

63 Ibid., 87.

64 Ibid., 100–02.

65 Ibid., 92–93, 96–98, 116.

66 "Replies," in *The Philosophy of W. V. Quine,* Library of Living Philosophers, Vol. 18, ed. Lewis Edwin Hahn and Paul Arthur Schilpp (Open Court, 1986), 663–65.

67 Harman, *The Nature of Morality*, 9–10.

68 Alfred North, *Process and Reality,* corrected edition, ed. David Ray Griffin and Donald W. Sherburne (The Free Press, 1978), 46.

69 Ibid., 40.

70 Alfred North Whitehead, *Adventures of Ideas* (The Free Press, 1967), 11, 277.

71 Whitehead, *Modes of Thought* (The Free Press 1968), 19; Whitehead, *Religion in the Making* (Fordham University Press, 1996 (reprint of 1926 edition), 60.

72 Whitehead, *Process and Reality*, 291.

73 Whitehead, *Science and the Modern World* (The Free Press 1967), 105. This passage reflects Whitehead's position when he delivered the Lowell Lectures, before he had developed his first doctrine of God, which is reflected in Chapters x and xi of that book.

74 Whitehead, *Adventures of Ideas*, 147, 168.

75 Whitehead, *Modes of Thought*, 103.

76 Whitehead, *Adventures of Ideas*, 36.

77 Ibid., 28–38.

78 Ibid., 86.

79 In evaluating this rational defense, one would, of course, need to examine the entire, thirteen-part cumulative case (see *Reenchantment without Supernaturalism*, Ch. 5), not simply the two parts discussed here. I later worked out this case more fully in *God Exists but Gawd Does Not: From Evil to New Atheism to Fine-Tuning* (Process Century Press, 2016).

CHAPTER FOUR

Religious Pluralism

RELIGIOUS PLURALISM, BESIDES BEING ONE OF THE CENTRAL ISSUES in contemporary religious thought, is also an issue to which process theology has made an especially important contribution. Although religious pluralism may arise as an issue in any of the religious traditions, most of the discussion of religious pluralism has occurred within the Christian tradition. Accordingly, I will, partly for this reason and partly for the sake of simplicity, deal with religious pluralism as it has been discussed by Christian theologians and by process Christian theologians in particular.[1]

I explain first what religious pluralism is and why it has arisen. I then discuss widespread criticisms of religious pluralism, pointing out that most of them are based on a version of religious pluralism that is very different from process theology's version. In the final section, I discuss this process version as pioneered by John B. Cobb, Jr., showing how it avoids the problems associated with the other version.

1 What Religious Pluralism Is

"Religious pluralism" is not simply the sociological fact that there are many different religions. That fact is usually called "religious diversity." To be a religious pluralist is to make two assertions. First, religious pluralists reject any *a priori* claim that their own religion is the only valid one.

For example, John Hick said that pluralism rejects the view that "there can be at most one true religion, in the sense of a religion teaching saving truth."[2] Pluralists are open in principle, in other words, to the possibility that other religions may be valid.

The second assertion goes beyond this mere statement of possibility to affirm that other religions are indeed valid, as when Christians, in Hick's words, assume that their "Jewish or Muslim or Hindu or Sikh or Buddhist friends and acquaintances are as fully entitled in the sight of God to live by their own religious traditions as we are to live by ours."[3]

To be a religious pluralist, therefore, is to reject absolutism, according to which one's own religion is considered the One True Way. The most severe form of Christian absolutism is *exclusivism*, according to which no one can be saved except through Christian faith. A less severe form of absolutism is *inclusivism*, which says that, although people in other religious traditions may be saved, they are saved only by virtue of God's saving act in Jesus Christ. The inclusivist, like the exclusivist, denies that other religions can be authentic paths to salvation.

The pluralist says that other religions can be authentic paths to salvation and that at least some of them are.[4]

2 Why Religious Pluralism Has Emerged

Religious pluralism, which has become an increasingly important factor since it began to emerge in the 17th and 18th centuries, has developed for at least five reasons: theological, ethical, sociological, scientific-philosophical, and dialogical.

The major *theological* motive has been the doctrine of divine love. John Hick said that he became a pluralist because he could not reconcile the idea that God is "infinite love" with the idea that "only by responding in faith to God in Christ can we be saved," because this would mean that "infinite love has ordained that human beings can be saved only in a way that in fact excludes the large majority of them."[5]

Catholic theologian Paul Knitter, having felt a tension "between two fundamental beliefs: God's universal love and desire to save, and the necessity of the church for salvation," decided that the doctrine of God's universal salvific will implies that the revelation given to others must be a potentially *saving* revelation, so that "Christians not only can but must look on other religions as possible *ways of salvation.*"[6]

The *ethical* motivation behind religious pluralism begins, Mark Heim observes, "with revulsion at the crimes of religious pride."[7] Illustrating this point, Hick devotes several pages to the "destructive effects of the assumption of Christian superiority," pointing out, for example, that "there is a clear connection between fifteen or so centuries of the 'absoluteness' of Christianity, with its corollary of the radical inferiority and perverseness of the Judaism it 'superseded,' and the consequent endemic anti-Semitism of Christian civilization," which led to the Holocaust.[8] If each religion could overcome its absoluteness "by the realization that one's own religion is one among several valid human responses to the Divine," Hick argues, "religion could become a healing instead of a divisive force in the world."[9]

These theological and ethical motivations for pluralism have been supported by a *sociological* fact about the modern world—that many Christians, through increased familiarity, are overcoming old stereotypes about other religions. Besides learning about these religions from books and mass media, Christians increasingly have neighbors belonging to other religious traditions. When they compare the lives of these people with that of fellow Christians, it becomes increasingly difficult to maintain the old view that the spiritual and moral fruits produced by Christianity prove it to be in a class by itself.[10]

Another external push toward pluralism has come from a *philosophical* result of the encounter with *modern science*. More important than any particular discovery or teaching of modern science is what can be called the scientific community's *presumption of naturalism*. Although sometimes the term "naturalism" is used to mean a materialistic, atheistic worldview, the basic meaning of naturalism—and the only meaning that science necessarily presupposes—is the denial of supernatural interruptions of the world's normal causal processes.[11] Much modern theology—that broad movement often called "liberal theology"—has accepted scientific naturalism in this sense. Hick, for example, says that the form of Christianity that "believed in miracles which arbitrarily disrupt the order of nature" is "incompatible with the scientific project."[12] This rejection of supernaturalism does not necessarily mean a rejection of theism. Many liberal theologians (including process theologians) have developed doctrines that can be called "theistic naturalism," or "naturalistic theism." This denial of supernatural interventions does not even entail that these theologians reject ongoing divine activity in the world (as process theologians especially show). But it does mean that they no longer assume that the founding events of Christian history involved a divine incursion into the world that was different in kind from the way that God works always and everywhere. For example, Ernst Troeltsch, the first major pluralist of the 20th century, rejected, in Knitter's words, "concepts of revelation that had God swooping down from heaven and intervening into history at particular spots."[13] Another major Christian pluralist, Wilfred Cantwell Smith, rejects the idea "that God has constructed Christianity" in favor of the idea that God "has inspired us to construct it, as He/She/It has inspired Muslims to construct what the world knows as Islam."[14]

The doctrinal revisions undertaken by pluralistic theologians have especially focused on traditional Christian theology's supernaturalistic christology. According to that christology, points out Hick, Jesus "was God—more precisely, God the Son, the second person of the Holy Trinity—incarnate," which implied "that Christianity, alone among the religions, was founded by God in person." Christianity was, therefore, "God's own religion in a sense in which no other can be."[15]

Process theologian John Cobb's first statement of his pluralistic position—which was entitled, significantly, *Christ in a Pluralistic Age*—rejected the traditional "supernaturalist and exclusivist" interpretation of the incarnation of the divine Logos in Jesus, according to which Jesus was "a supernatural being," namely, "the transcendent, omnipotent, omniscient ruler of the world . . . walking about on earth in human form."[16]

The rejection of supernaturalism applies also to the traditional idea of salvation, according to which it involves a divine decision, based on arbitrary standards, that saves some people from eternal damnation. Recognizing that Christian exclusivism and inclusivism both depend on some such definition of salvation, such as "being forgiven and accepted by God because of the atoning death of Jesus," Hick suggests that "we define salvation . . . as an actual change in human beings," which involves "a long process," not a sudden, supernaturally effected transformation.[17] Cobb, likewise, speaks of "salvation as something we participate in here and now rather than, or in addition to, life beyond."[18]

A fifth motivation behind the development of pluralistic forms of Christian theology has been what some have called the *dialogical* imperative.[19] This imperative has both ethical and theological motivations. The major *ethical* motivation is the recognition that many of the problems of our planet are so great that they can be overcome, if at all, only through the cooperation of the world's various religions. Knitter, for example, argues that all the religions today are facing the human demand for "some form of this-worldly, earthly (as opposed to purely spiritual) *liberation*," so that "*liberation*—what it is and how to achieve it—constitutes a new arena for the encounter of religions."[20]

The major *theological* motive for dialogue is that, once we see that our own religion is not the one and only true religion, we realize that other traditions may have truths and values that are not provided, at least as clearly, in our own religion. The conclusion that Christianity, like every other religion, is limited, says Knitter, leads to the dialogical imperative, because it is through dialogue with members of other religious traditions that "we can expand or correct the truth that we have," thereby overcoming the "limitations of our own viewpoint."[21] This motive, as we will see, is central to Cobb's pluralistic theology.

3 Criticisms of Religious Pluralism

Although for many theologians, the need for Christianity to embrace pluralism is now beyond question, not all theologians agree. From the perspective of many Christian thinkers, "Christian pluralism" is a self-contradiction. One cannot hold Christian faith in an authentic form, they believe, and be a pluralist. Much of this rejection of Christian pluralism arises from an absolutist, supernaturalist notion of Christian faith, which simply presupposes that the only authentic form of Christian faith is one that assumes, *a priori*, that it is the only religion sanctioned by God.

This kind of criticism can be largely ignored by pluralists, because the controversy is not about pluralism as such but about the proper Christian response to modern thought — whether the liberal rejection of the supernaturalist framework is a necessary adjustment by Christian faith or a betrayal of that faith.

There is another criticism, however, that must be taken more seriously. According to this criticism, pluralism inevitably leads to a kind of relativism that is antithetical to Christian faith. The centrality of this issue was pointed out in a landmark book by Alan Race, who said: "The pertinent question mark which hovers over all theories of pluralism is how far they succeed in overcoming the sense of 'debilitating relativism' which is their apparent danger." By "debilitating relativism," Race meant the view that all religions are equally true in a way that makes them equally false.[22]

At least one pluralist theologian, Langdon Gilkey, believed that this danger cannot be avoided. Seeing "no consistent theological way to relativize and yet to assert our own symbols," Gilkey concluded that giving up our absolute starting point leads to an "unavoidable relativism."[23]

The reason this concern looms so large is not only the fact that the way to affirm pluralism without relativism is not immediately obvious, but also the fact that some of the most prominent pluralists have been led to relativism. For example, Ernst Troeltsch has been called not only the first great Christian pluralist but also "the first great Christian relativist."[24] And the position of John Hick has been widely criticized as leading to a complete relativism. This fact is of great significance because Hick's version of pluralism, besides being the version that has been discussed far more than any other,[25] is widely taken as representative of pluralism as such.

For example, Kevin Meeker and Philip Quinn said that they reserved the term *religious pluralism* "to refer to the position John Hick adopts in response to the fact of religious diversity."[26] Mark Heim, seeing Hick as having made "the philosophical case for a pluralistic outlook," treated Hick's position as the paradigmatic pluralistic theology.[27] Any weaknesses in Hick's position, therefore, have widely been taken to be weaknesses of pluralism as such. It is, accordingly, important to see that the weaknesses in Hick's position, which have led to such widespread criticism, follow from his particular version of pluralism, rather than from pluralism as such.

Although Hick's move to pluralism began, as we saw, with his conviction about what the divine love would not do, the particular way Hick worked out his pluralistic position led him to the conclusion that personalistic words such as "love" could not be applied to the Divine Reality in itself. What led Hick to this conclusion was a fact combined with an assumption. The fact was that the reports of profound religious (mystical) experience can be divided into at least two major types: those that describe communion with a good, loving, personal deity, distinct from the experiencer, and those that describe a realization of identity with ultimate reality experienced as formless, impersonal, ineffable, and "beyond good and evil." The existence of these two types of religious experience creates a problem in part because they are both reported, as Caroline Franks Davis points out, as apprehensions of "the nature of *ultimate* reality."[28]

But this fact would not have created a problem except for a crucial assumption on Hick's part. This assumption was that, as Cobb put it critically, "what is approached as 'ultimate reality' must be one and the same."[29] As Hick himself put it, "there cannot be a plurality of ultimates."[30] Given that assumption, Hick faced a serious question, which is, in Davis's words:

> How can "ultimate reality" be both a personal being and an impersonal principle, identical to our inmost self and forever "other," loving and utterly indifferent, good and amoral, knowable and unknowable, a plenitude and "emptiness"?[31]

Hick, in seeking to answer this question, decided that as a pluralist he could not play favorites by saying that the one kind of religious experience was more authentic—more revelatory of ultimate reality—than the other. He decided, accordingly, that ultimate reality in itself—which he often calls simply the "Real in itself"—must be considered completely unknowable (like Immanuel Kant's "noumenal reality"), and must, therefore, be distinguished from all human ideas about ultimate reality.

These human ideas are then divided into two types: divine *personae*, such as the biblical God and Advaita Vedanta's saguna Brahman (Brahman with qualities), and the *impersonae*, such as Advaita Vedanta's nirguna Brahman (Brahman without qualities) and Buddhism's "Sunyata" (usually translated "emptiness"). None of these human ideas about ultimate reality correspond to the ultimate reality in itself, said Hick, because the Real in itself "cannot be said to be one or many, person or thing, substance or process, good or evil, purposive or non-purposive."[32] Therefore, Hick said, we cannot apply to ultimate reality in itself any substantive predicates, such as "being good," "being powerful," and "having knowledge."[33]

Hick's position thereby does lead to the "debilitating relativism" of which Alan Race spoke. In his eagerness to show all religions to be equally true, Hick in effect declared them all to be equally false, thereby undercutting their support for moral and spiritual attitudes. Hick did, to be sure, claim that "the major world religions constitute varying human responses to the transcendent Reality, and are thus at least to some extent *in alignment with that Reality*," so that they can to that extent provide criteria for valuing various human attitudes.[34] For example, pointing out that saints in all religious traditions manifest "compassion/love towards other human beings or towards all life,"[35] Hick implied that this attitude is in alignment with "transcendent Reality."

However, given Hick's assertion that this "transcendent Reality" is entirely devoid of purpose, goodness, compassion, and love, he could not legitimately say that the saint's "compassion/love" is any more in alignment with it than Hitler's hate and indifference. Hick's version of religious pluralism is widely rejected because of this complete undermining of Christian faith and ethics.[36]

Another widespread criticism is that Hick's so-called pluralistic position was not really pluralistic. This criticism is based on the fact that Hick said not only that all religions are oriented toward the same ultimate reality but also that they all aim at essentially the same "salvation," which Hick described as a "transformation of human existence from self-centredness to Reality-centredness."[37] One problem created by this lack of genuine pluralism, Heim pointed out, is that by implying that "the specific and special aspects of another faith tell us [nothing] that is of significant importance," it provides no motivation for dialogue.[38]

Heim's equation of pluralism with Hick's specific version of it is shown by his comment that "the pluralistic hypothesis" rests on two dubious assumptions: "a metaphysical dogma that there can be but one religious object, and a soteriological dogma that there can

be but one religious end."[39] By virtue of thereby equating pluralism
with Hick's position, Heim ends up with a paradoxical position. On
the one hand, saying that, "Despite their appropriation of the title,
['pluralistic'] theologies are not religiously pluralistic at all," Heim
argued that we need a "truly pluralistic hypothesis."[40]

On the other hand, repeatedly referring negatively to "pluralism"
and "pluralistic theology,"[41] he called for a "post-pluralistic" theology.[42]
This second conclusion—which came through as his book's dominant
message[43]—reinforces the view of others who have used the problems
inherent in Hick's version of pluralistic theology to call for leaving
pluralistic theology as such behind.[44]

4 Process Theology's Complementary Religious Pluralism

Whitehead's process philosophy provides the basis for a different
version of religious pluralism. Two features of Whitehead's philosophy
are especially relevant. One of these was his concern, in dealing with
different systems of thought, to show how assertions that at first sight
appear to be *contradictory* may actually express *complementary* truths.
Whitehead suggested this approach with regard to science and religion,
saying that a clash between their teachings is "a sign that there are
wider truths . . . within which a reconciliation of a deeper religion
and a more subtle science will be found."[45]

He also suggested it with regard to Buddhism and Christianity,
saying that instead of sheltering themselves from each other, they
should "look[] to each other for deeper meanings." In each case, the
task is to overcome formulations that, while expressing a measure of
truth, have done so in "over-assertive" ways, "thereby implying an
exclusion of complementary truths."[46]

The other feature of Whitehead's philosophy that is especially
germane to pluralism is his view of the relation between God and
creativity. "Creativity," which involves a generalization of the physicist's
"energy," refers to the power embodied in all actual things—both
God and finite actualities.

According to Whitehead's view of actual entities, they are momentary "actual occasions," which come into existence out of the causal influence of the past, exercise a degree of self-determination, and then come to completion, after which they exert causal influence on future actual occasions. Your experience during a few seconds, for example, is composed of a number of actual occasions—also called "occasions of experience."

Whitehead's term "creativity" points to the twofold power of each occasion of experience to exert a degree of self-determination in forming itself and then to exert causal influence on the future. Whitehead's term "creativity" thus provides a new understanding of what previous philosophers have simply called "being" or "being itself," and which theologian Paul Tillich called "the power of being." But for Whitehead, unlike Tillich, God is not simply being itself, understood as the power of being, but the ultimate *embodiment* of this power.

The distinctive feature of Whitehead's position is that God and creaturely creativity are equally primordial. Although traditional theologians regarded the power to create as eternal, this power belonged to God alone—the fact that a world with its own power exists was due to a voluntary divine decision. This idea was enshrined in the doctrine of *creatio ex nihilo*, according to which our world was created out of a complete absence of finite actual entities. Whitehead rejected this doctrine, suggesting instead that our world was created—as the Bible itself suggests[47]—out of a primeval chaos.

Although our particular world is a contingent divine creation, there has always been *a* world, in the sense of a multiplicity of finite actualities embodying creativity, and therefore the twofold power of exerting self-determination and exerting causal influence on other things. To say that God has always co-existed with creativity, therefore, means that creativity has always been embodied in a world as well as in God—that there has always been worldly creativity as well as divine creativity.

This doctrine is doubly important for the issue of religious pluralism. In the first place, this doctrine explains the impossibility of supernatural interruptions. Traditional theism's supernaturalism was undergirded by its doctrine of *creatio ex nihilo*. By saying that the very fact that there is a finite world at all is due to God's free decision, traditional theists implied that all the principles embodied in our world—not only what we call the "laws of nature" but also the most fundamental causal principles—were freely created. And what was freely created could be freely interrupted.

This doctrine, besides giving traditional theists an insoluble problem of evil,[48] also lay behind their absolutist view that Christianity is the only divinely ordained religion. Thanks to supernatural intervention, the fallibility that is involved in all human thinking could have been divinely overcome in the case of the authors of the New Testament, resulting in an infallibly inspired book.

Process theologian Marjorie Suchocki has developed the implications of this Whiteheadian view of the God-world relation in her highly readable book, *Divinity and Diversity*, which is subtitled *A Christian Affirmation of Religious Pluralism*. Because all creatures have their own creativity, hence their own freedom of response—as the creation narrative in Genesis itself suggests—God's activity in the world must take the form of "call and response."

Because the various creatures will often use their freedom to respond in different ways, diversity arises. God's call at any time will be relevant to the responses previously made by a particular species, or a particular religious tradition. Accordingly, Suchocki concluded:

> If God works through call and response, and if human freedom introduces variety into the response, then shouldn't we expect to find different stories, rituals, orders of social structure, and senses of the sacred, but all tending toward creating the good within human forms of community?[49]

In developing the implications of this view for the Christian understanding of the "reign of God," she said that we are today called to
this task:

> [T]o live a reign of God that reaches not toward an imperialism
> of one religion—our own!—sweeping the planet, but that
> reaches toward a new form of community: a community
> made up of diverse religious communities, existing together
> in friendship.[50]

Equally important for religious pluralism is the fact that the distinction between God and creativity provides a basis for speaking of
two ultimates. This idea has been most fully worked out by John Cobb,
whose position, in contrast with Hick's identist pluralism, can be
called "complementary pluralism."[51] Different religions, Cobb holds,
have seen different truths and have offered different paths to salvation.

In developing the idea that there are two ultimates, Cobb suggested
that one of these, corresponding with Whitehead's "creativity," has
been called "Emptiness" ("*Sunyata*") or "Dharmakaya" by Buddhists,
"nirguna Brahman" by Advaita Vedantists, "the Godhead" by Meister
Eckhart, and "Being Itself" by Heidegger and Tillich. It is the *formless*
ultimate.

The other ultimate, corresponding with what Whitehead calls
"God," is not Being Itself but the *Supreme* Being. Far from being
formless, it is the world's source of all forms, such as truth, beauty,
and justice. It has been called "Amida Buddha" or "Sambhogakaya,"
"saguna Brahman," "Ishvara," "Yahweh," "Christ," and "Allah."[52]

In Cobb's view, there are good reasons to prefer this hypothesis
to Hick's. One reason is that it is simply not illuminating to say that
God, who is *worshipped*, and Emptiness, which is *realized*, are "two
names for the same noumenal reality."[53] Cobb's hypothesis allows us
to recognize them as the different realities they seem to be. A second
advantage of this alternative hypothesis, Cobb said, is that it allows
Christian theologians to avoid the "relativization and even negation
of basic Christian commitments" implicit in Hick's hypothesis.[54]

"[T]hose who assume that all traditions must be focusing on the same aspects of reality," Cobb said, are led to believe that what Zen Buddhists call Emptying "must be the same as God," which can in turn lead the Christian thinker to "employ the negative theology on the Christian heritage so radically as to dissolve God into Emptying. In that process everything distinctive of the biblical heritage is lost."[55]

Whiteheadian pluralists, by contrast, can affirm the existence of a Divine Actuality with many characteristics in common with the biblical God, including those that support the concern for a just social order, without disagreeing with the description, provided by nontheistic Hindus and Buddhists, of ultimate reality as formless. Finally, Cobb said, "When we understand global religious experience and thought in this way, it is easier to view the contributions of diverse traditions as complementary."[56]

This last point is crucial, given Cobb's view that the challenge of interreligious dialogue is "to transform contradictory statements into different but not contradictory ones," thereby moving "toward a more comprehensive vision in which the deepest insights of both sides are reconciled."[57] One basis for such reconciliation is to recognize that claims that may at first glance seem contradictory are really answers to different questions. "[T]here is no contradiction in the claim of one that problem A is solved by X and the claim of the other that problem B is solved by Y. . . . The claims are complementary rather than contradictory."[58] For example:

> Consider the Buddhist claim that Gautama is the Buddha. That is a very different statement from the assertion that God was incarnate in Jesus. The Buddha is the one who is enlightened. To be enlightened is to realize the fundamental nature of reality, its insubstantiality, its relativity, its emptiness. . . . That Jesus was the incarnation of God does not deny that Gautama was the Enlightened One.[59]

Another example involves the tension between the Christian assertion "that Jesus is the Christ" and the Jewish insistence "that the Messiah has not come." Jews and Christians, Cobb suggests, should "work together repeatedly to clarify the difference between what Jews mean by 'Messiah' and what Christians legitimately mean by 'Christ.'"[60]

In his landmark book on religious pluralism, Alan Race, after warning of the danger of "debilitating relativism," pointed to Cobb's version as an exception. "The virtue of Cobb's contribution," said Race, "is that he combines fidelity to Christ with unqualified openness to other faiths."[61] Cobb illustrated this assessment by saying that, to enter into interreligious dialogue, "we do not need to relativize our beliefs. . . . We can affirm our insights as universally valid! What we cannot do, without lapsing back into unjustified arrogance, is to deny that the insights of other traditions are also universally valid."[62]

Notes

1   For examples of Jewish, Muslim, and Buddhist process pluralism, respectively, see Sandra B. Lubarsky, *Tolerance and Transformation: Jewish Approaches to Religious Pluralism* (Hebrew Union College Press, 1990); Sir Mohammad Iqbal, *The Reconstruction of Religious Thought in Islam* (Oxford University Press, 1934); and Ryusei Takeda, "Mutual Transformation of Pure Land Buddhism and Christianity: Methodology and Possibilities in the Light of Shinran's Doctrine," *Bulletin of the Nanzan Institute for Religion and Culture* 22 (Spring 1998), 6–40.

2   John Hick, *A Christian Theology of Religions: The Rainbow of Faiths* (Westminster John Knox, 1995), 24.

3   Ibid., 125.

4   This typology of exclusivism, inclusivism, and pluralism was introduced by Alan Race in *Christians and Religious Pluralism: Patterns in Christian Theology of Religions* (Orbis, 1983).

5   John Hick, *Philosophy of Religion*, 3rd edition (Prentice-Hall, 1983), 117–18.

6   Paul F. Knitter, *No Other Name? A Critical Survey of Christian*

Attitudes Toward the World Religions (Orbis, 1985), 121, 125, 116–17, 140.

7   Mark S. Heim, *Salvations: Truth and Difference in Religion* (Orbis, 1995), 72.

8   John Hick, "The Non-Absoluteness of Christianity," in John Hick and Paul F. Knitter, eds., *The Myth of Christian Uniqueness: Toward a Pluralistic Theology of Religions* (Orbis, 1987), 16–36, at 18.

9   Hick, *Christian Theology of Religions*, 123.

10 Ibid., 13.

11 I develop this point in *Religion and Scientific Naturalism: Overcoming the Conflicts* (State University of New York Press, 2000).

12 Hick, *Christian Theology of Religions*, 53.

13 Knitter, *No Other Name*, 25.

14 Smith, "Idolatry in Comparative Perspective," in Hick and Knitter, eds., *Myth of Christian Uniquenes*, 53–68, at 59.

15 Hick, *Christian Theology of Religions*, 15.

16 John B. Cobb, Jr., *Christ in a Pluralistic Age* (Westminster, 1975), 27, 163.

17 Hick, *Christian Theology of Religions*, 16–18.

18 Cobb, in Leonard Swidler, John B. Cobb, Jr., Paul F. Knitter, and Monica K. Hellwig, *Death or Dialogue? From the Age of Monologue to the Age of Dialogue* (1Trinity Press; London: SCM Press, 1990), 1–18, at 13.

19 David Lochhead, *The Dialogical Imperative: A Christian Reflection on Interfaith Encounter* (Orbis, 1988).

20 Knitter, "Interreligious Dialogue: What? Why? How?" in Swidler et al., *Death or Dialogue*, 19–44, at 27.

21 Knitter, *No Other Name*, 36; *Jesus and the Other Names: Christian Mission and Global Responsibility* (Orbis, 1996), 29, 31.

22 Race, *Christians and Religious Pluralism*, 90, 78.

23 Langdon Gilkey, "Plurality and Its Theological Implications," in Hick and Knitter, eds., *Myth of Christian Uniquenes*, 37–53, at 44–46.

24 Cobb, *Beyond Dialogue: Toward a Mutual Transformation of Buddhism and Christianity* (Fortress, 1982), 13.

25 When Hick's *Christian Theologyo of Religions* was published in 1995, a bibliography of critiques of his position filled almost five pages.

26 Kevin Meeker and Philip L. Quinn, "Introduction: The Philosophical Challenge of Religious Diversity," in Quinn and Meeker, eds., *The Philosophical Challenge of Religious Diversity*, 1–28, at 3.

27 Heim, *Salvations*, 8, 42.

28 Caroline Franks Davis, *The Evidential Force of Religious Experience* (Clarendon Press, 1989), 167.

29 Cobb, *Beyond Dialogue*, 96.

30 Hick, *An Interpretation of Religion* (Yale University Press, 1989), 249.

31 Davis, *The Evidential Force of Religious Experience*, 172–73.

32 Hick, *An Interpretation of Religion*, 245.

33 Ibid., 239.

34 Ibid., 300; emphasis added.

35 Ibid., 301.

36 For negative critiques of Hick's position, see Heim, *Salvations*; Quinn and Meeker, eds., *The Philosophical Challenge of Religious Diversity*; and Gavin D'Costa, ed., *Christian Uniqueness Reconsidered: The Myth of a Pluralistic Theology of Religions* (Orbis, 1990).

37 Hick, *An Interpretation of Religion*, 300.

38 Heim, *Salvations*, 125. The criticism that Hick's position is "not really pluralistic" is somewhat misleading, because Hick does affirm pluralism as defined in the first section. But Hick's position, by virtue of affirming that all religions are oriented to an identical ultimate and aim at an identical salvation, can be called "identist pluralism."

39 Ibid., 23.

40. Ibid., 129-30.

41 Ibid., 16, 87, 88, 89, 90, 101, 103, 109, 125, 129, 130, 228.

42 Ibid., 226.

43 This is suggested by the fact that Paul J. Griffiths' rave review of the book is titled "Beyond Pluralism" (*First Things*, January 1996: 50–52).

44 Gavin D'Costa, having criticized the pluralist project as defined in Hick and Knitter's *Myth of Christian Uniqueness*, questions "whether 'pluralistic theology' is an appropriate or even adequate interpretation of religious plurality" (*Christian Uniqueness Reconsidered*, x–xi). See also Paul Griffiths' review in the previous note.

45 Alfred North Whitehead, *Science and the Modern World* (The Free Press, 1967), 185.

46 Whitehead, *Religion in the Making* (Macmillan, 1926; Fordham University Press, 1996), 146, 145, 149.

47 Although it has widely been assumed that the Bible teaches creation out of nothing, this doctrine did not arise until near the end of the second century of Christian thought. See my "Creation out of Nothing, Creation Out of Chaos, and the Problem of Evil," *Encountering Evil: Live Options in Theodicy*, 2nd edition, ed. Stephen T. Davis (Westminster/John Knox, 2001), 108–25.

48 See, besides the essay mentioned in the previous note, my *God, Power, and Evil: A Process Theodicy* (Westminster Press, 1976 (reprinted with a new preface, University Press of America, 1991), and *Evil Revisited: Responses and Reconsiderations* (State University of New York Press, 1991).

49 Marjorie Hewitt Suchocki, *Divinity and Diversity: A Christian Affirmation of Religious Pluralism* (Abingdon Press, 2003), 29–35.

50 Ibid., 86.

51 See note 38, above.

52 Cobb, 116; *Beyond Dialogue*, 124–28; *Transforming Christianity and the World: A Way beyond Absolutism and Relativism*, ed. Paul F. Knitter (Orbis, 1999), 184–85.

53 Cobb, *Beyond Dialogue*, 43.

54 Cobb, *Transforming Christianity and the World*, 79.

55 Cobb, *Death or Dialogue*, 6.

56 Cobb, *Transforming Christianity and the World*, 186.

57 Ibid., 74; *Death or Dialogue,* 120.

58 Ibid., 14.

59 Cobb, *Transforming Christianity and the World,* 140.

60 Ibid., 86–87.

61 Race, *Christians and Religious Pluralism*, 98.

62 Cobb, *Transforming Christianity and the World,* 137.

CHAPTER FIVE

Process Eschatology

I N THIS ESSAY, I DISCUSS ESCHATOLOGY from the perspective of process theology. As pointed out in this book's first paragraph, the term "process theology" can be used more widely, but it is usually, as here, understood as the theological movement that employs the "process philosophy" of Alfred North Whitehead and Charles Hartshorne.

Process theology in this sense generally involves two aspects: the employment of Whiteheadian and/or Hartshornean philosophy as a philosophical theology, and the use of this philosophical theology in articulating the doctrines of a particular religious tradition. I am here writing as a Christian process theologian. As such, I take seriously the question whether process theology can do justice to the basic dimensions of the eschatology of Jesus.

Salvation for Jesus involved four dimensions: (1) salvation from the threat of meaninglessness through confidence that we are known and loved by our creator; (2) an ultimate salvation in a resurrected life beyond bodily death; (3) a salvation that would be realized on earth with the coming political reign of God; and (4) a reign of God in the individual heart and in social relations (which is made possible by belief in the first three dimensions of salvation).

Modern liberal theology has generally denied the second and third dimensions and sometimes even the first, thereby leaving the fourth dimension — often called "realized eschatology" — with little if any basis.

Process theology has often been considered an example of this modern liberal theology, especially with regard to the question of eschatology. It is certainly true that some process theologians have affirmed only the first dimension as a basis for the fourth. Some critics, furthermore, have assumed that this extremely limited eschatology is inherent in process theology as such, given its denial of omnipotence in the traditional sense. Anglican theologian Austin Farrer, for example, complained that the God of process theism is "human enough to have a natural need of his creatures" but *not* "divine enough to save their souls alive."[1]

I will show, however, that process theology has the resources to affirm all four dimensions of the eschatology of Jesus and that some process theologians do make these affirmations. I will refer to the four dimensions of salvation discussed above as salvation$_1$, salvation$_2$, salvation$_3$, and salvation$_4$, respectively.

1 Salvation$_1$

Salvation$_1$, the peace that can come from confidence that our lives are ultimately meaningful because they are cherished everlastingly by our creator, is affirmed by all process theologians, starting with Whitehead and Hartshorne themselves.

Whitehead affirmed this notion in terms of "objective immortality." Explaining this technical term requires introducing some others.

Every enduring individual, such as the human mind or soul, is said to be a serially ordered society of momentary "occasions of experience." Each such occasion begins as a subject enjoying "subjective immediacy." When it reaches "satisfaction," its subjective immediacy "perishes."

This occasion of experience is now an object for future subjects, which "prehend" it, thereby taking it into themselves. Each occasion, therefore, first exists for itself, as a subject, and then exists as an object in succeeding subjects. This existence in later subjects gives it "objective immortality."

It is important to understand precisely how the terms "object" and "objective" are used. To say that something is an "object" does not necessarily mean that it is a "mere object" in the sense of something devoid of experience. "Object" is a relative term, meaning only that the thing in question is *the object of some subject's experience.* And in some cases an object in this sense is an-object-that-had-itself-been-a-subject.

Such is the case when I remember a previous occasion of my own experience. That previous occasion no longer enjoys subjective immediacy, because that experiencing is no longer going on. When I remember it, it exists in my present experience, but not subjectively, as an experiencing subject, but only objectively, as an object of my present experience.

I do not, however, experience this object in the same way as I experience objects such as rocks, stars, and the number 4, which I can perceive with indifference. Rather, I take that object-that-had-itself-been-a-subject into my present experience by feeling *its* feelings. For it to be "objectified," therefore, is for its experience to be retained in my present experience, albeit partly. And it is then retained, to a lesser degree, in all succeeding moments of my experience. In this sense it has "objective immortality."

However, besides the fact that this immortality is only objective, it is also very limited. As indicated by the qualifications—"albeit partly," "to a lesser degree"—our present experience never perfectly retains past experiences. As Whitehead put it: "Objectification involves elimination. . . . [T]the past is present under an abstraction." He added, however, that "there is no reason, of any ultimate meta-physical generality, why this should be the whole story."[2]

The other part of the story is supplied by his doctrine of God's "consequent nature." Contrasted with God's "primordial nature," which refers to God's primordial envisagement of eternal possibilities through which God influences the world, the "consequent nature" refers to God as consequent upon — responsive to — the world of flux. "The consequent nature of God is the fluent world become 'everlasting' by its objective immortality in God."[3] Objective immortality in God is different from objective immortality within the finite world — often called "social immortality" — because in God's objectification of the world "there is no loss."[4]

For Whitehead, this doctrine provided an answer to what he saw as the "ultimate evil in the temporal world," which is "deeper than any specific evil," this being "the fact that the past fades" as time moves on. Our present efforts seem important to us now, but how important will they seem to people 100 or 1,000 years from now? Most of us will not even merit a footnote in the history books of the future. "Yet the culminating fact of conscious, rational life refuses to conceive of itself as a transient enjoyment, transiently useful."[5]

We human beings, in other words, have a demand for *meaning*, to believe that our lives are somehow *permanently* useful, making a permanent contribution, so that reality will never be as if we had not existed. Seeing this as the "problem set by the penetration of the finer religious intuition," Whitehead regarded "everlastingness" as "the content of that vision upon which the finer religions are built — the 'many' absorbed everlastingly in the final unity."[6]

Hartshorne saw the ultimate human problem similarly, pointing out that even when we are successful in achieving our aims, reflection about the long-term future raises the question whether our struggles really will make any ultimate difference. "Be the aim Nirvana, the Classless Society, the Welfare State, Self-realization," said Hartshorne, "the query is never silenced, what good is it, from the cosmic and everlasting perspective, that one or the other or all of these aims be attained for a time on this ball of rock?"[7]

The ultimate meaning of life, he argued, could be secured only through our immortality in the divine experience, which is, qualitatively different from our experience in the sense of being all-inclusive and all-retaining:

> Deity is the highest possible form of the inclusion of others in the self. . . . Infallibly and with unrivaled adequacy aware of all others, God includes others—not, as we do, in a mostly indistinct or largely unconscious manner, but with full clarity. . . . Since God forgets nothing, loses no value once acquired, our entire worth is imperishable in the divine life.[8]

This objective immortality is the only type of which Hartshorne spoke. He even explicitly denied "immortality as [an infinite] career after death . . . in which our individual consciousnesses will have *new* experiences not enjoyed or suffered while on earth."[9]

Hartshorne regarded this denial as important theologically, because belief in our own subjective immortality tended, he thought, "to make God a mere means for our everlasting happiness," whereas the true meaning of life is that we are privileged to contribute to the life of God, "the only immortal being."[10]

Some Christian process theologians have followed Hartshorne on this point. Schubert Ogden, for example, said in an early essay on eschatology that he neither accepted, nor considered essential to Christian faith, the view that we "continue to exist as experiencing subjects" after bodily death.[11] Although Ogden did not rule out the possibility of life after death, his attitude was made clear in a later statement that, "Whether or not we somehow manage to survive death for a longer or shorter period of time, I regard as a question of no particular theological interest."[12]

This Hartshorne-Ogden view, which treats what many Christians consider to be an essential dimension of Christian faith as a matter of indifference as well as probably false, has sometimes been taken to be the position of process theology as such. For example, Austin Farrer said of his attack on process theology, "The Prior Actuality of God," that he "wrote it in a rage" after reading some of Ogden's writings.[13] Process theology, however, has other options.

2 Salvation₂

Some process theologians do not treat the idea of continued experiencing after bodily death as a matter of indifference. For example, in an essay entitled "The Resurrection of the Soul," John B. Cobb, Jr., having pointed to the widespread tendency by theologians to limit their discussion of the resurrection to its "symbolic value" or "existential meaning," added:

> Yet the question of what, if anything, happens after we die has not disappeared from the range of human concerns. It has simply moved out of professional theology into other hands. Our sophisticated equivocations on this topic have contributed to our general irrelevance to the religious interests of our contemporaries.[14]

Marjorie Suchocki, arguing that the doctrine of objective immortality is not sufficient "for those who have been broken by evil,"[15] has asserted that "the Christian hope for God's final victory over evil" requires a doctrine of *subjective* immortality.[16]

I myself argued that distinctively human problems associated with our anticipation of death—our awareness of the injustice of this life, our longing for more life, and our desire for wholeness—mean that the doctrine of objective immortality is, while extremely important, insufficient.[17]

It is, of course, one thing to say this. It is another to show how something more can be intelligibly affirmed. The primary reason why some process theologians, like many other theologians in recent times, have not affirmed salvation₂ is the widespread belief that our continuation as experiencing subjects after bodily death is impossible. Process theologians have responded to this problem in two different ways. One way, taken by Marjorie Suchocki, was to accept this conclusion but argue that Whitehead's philosophy nevertheless allows for a kind of subjective immortality.

SUBJECTIVE IMMORTALITY OF EXPERIENCES

At the root of Suchocki's argument was the claim that the reason an occasion of experience is present only *objectively*, rather than as an experiencing subject, in subsequent occasions is *not* because an occasion can be prehended only after its subjectivity has perished—as most Whitehead scholars have taken him to say—but only because of the finitude of finite prehenders.

Arguing that "the satisfaction allows either subjective or objective prehension," she asserted: "Whether a prehension is objective or subjective depends not upon the satisfaction, but upon the prehending entity." Finite entities can prehend a past occasion only partially, so they must abstract from its subjective unity and hence its subjectivity, but God "prehends the satisfaction's entirety, and hence its subjectivity." Accordingly, "the occasion would be subjectively immortal in God."[18] God's prehension of our successive occasions of experience, therefore, effects their "resurrection" into the divine life.[19]

It should be noted that this is a doctrine of subjective immortality not primarily for souls but for individual occasions of experience—Suchocki spoke of "resurrected occasions of experience."[20] It is not uniquely relevant, therefore, to our existence after bodily death but applies all the time. And this resurrection is not simply for human occasions but is for all occasions of experience whatsoever, from the human to the subatomic level. Every occasion, Suchocki said, becomes immortal—"objectively in finite occasions, and subjectively in God."[21] Suchocki's emphasis, nevertheless, is on the implications of this doctrine for human beings. Subjective immortality in God provides the basis for God to overcome all the evils of human history.

Up to this point, Suchocki could well claim that her modification of Whiteheadian metaphysics is minor and even that it was partly anticipated by Whitehead and Hartshorne themselves.[22] Her suggestion of how evil is overcome in God led her, however, to modify their positions much more drastically.

Her radical modification allows the divinely prehended occasion, besides retaining its subjective immediacy, to have new experiences: "it will feel its own immediacy, and God's feeling of its immediacy as well."[23] Furthermore, by virtue of its "participat[ion] in the consciousness of God, . . . the occasion will feel all others, and therefore will experience itself from the perspective of those others."[24] Through this transformation of each occasion, Suchocki argued, each occasion, and hence each person, can experience both final judgment and ultimate redemption.[25]

I have argued elsewhere that Suchocki's position involves violations of basic Whiteheadian categories, especially in allowing an occasion of experience to have additional experiences after it has reached satisfaction.[26] Suchocki recognized this problem, pointing out that "it is axiomatic that the 'satisfaction' of a subject . . . can sustain no addition" and that "[b]y definition, the immediacy contained in the finite satisfaction cannot be increased."[27] Her position, however, did require each occasion to have further experiences after it is prehended by God.

It appears that Suchocki was led into this contradiction by trying to see how God might overcome the injustices of history on the assumption that the traditional way of envisaging this—with individuals experiencing purgation, sanctification, and reconciliation in a life that continues beyond bodily death—can no longer be affirmed. Other process theologians, however, have pointed out that Whitehead's philosophy does allow that traditional notion of life after death to be reaffirmed.

LIFE AFTER DEATH RULED OUT BY MATERIALISM
AND EPIPHENOMENALISM

The main reason for the denial of life after death in late modern thought is the rejection of supernaturalism combined with the acceptance of a view of the mind-body relation — either material-ism or epiphenomenalism — that makes the mind's existence apart from the brain seem impossible.

- According to materialism, what we call the mind — with its experience — is not some entity distinct from the brain but is in some sense identical with it. Materialists, in fact, often call their position "identism."

- Epiphenomenalists, not seeing how experiences can be prop-erties of a material object — even one as complex as a human brain — regard the mind as a nonefficacious byproduct of the brain's functioning. Although the mind is distinct from the brain, it has no power of its own.

Neither materialists nor epiphenomenalists regard the mind, accord-ingly, as an entity that could conceivably exist apart from the physical body. Given this view, life beyond bodily death would be possible only if the physical body were to be resurrected.[28] But such a resurrection, requiring the agency of a being with omnipotence in the traditional sense, is ruled out by the rejection of supernaturalism. The idea of life after death cannot, therefore, be taken seriously.

Although Whitehead himself never in his writings affirmed life after death (as distinct from objective immortality), he did acknowledge that his philosophical position made it *possible*. In 1926, he wrote that his philosophy "is entirely neutral on the question of immortality, or on the existence of purely spiritual beings other than God."[29] Being neutral meant that it made life after death neither necessary nor impossible.

Whitehead's openness to this possibility may reflect the in-fluence of J. M. E. McTaggart, who was one of Whitehead's closest philosophical friends.[30] McTaggart provided an answer to the ar-gument that the entirely brain-dependent nature of the mind — and hence epiphenomenalism if not materialism — is proved by empirical facts, especially the fact that damage to the brain results in derangement, loss of various cognitive abilities, or even complete loss of consciousness. Such facts, McTaggart pointed out, support only the proposition that *"while a self has a body,* that body is essentially connected with the self's mental life." For example, "the fact that an abnormal state of the brain may affect our thoughts does not prove that the normal states of the brain are necessary for thought."[31]

Although Whitehead did not explicitly endorse McTaggart's position on this issue, at least in print, it is consistent with a statement in one of his last writings. Having defined the human soul as "a personal living society of high-grade occasions," Whitehead added:

> How far this soul finds a support for its existence beyond the body is:—another question. . . . [I]n some important sense the existence of the soul may be freed from its complete dependence upon the bodily organization.[32]

To understand how Whitehead could say this while rejecting supernaturalism, it is necessary to see how his position on the mind-body relation differs from the both dualism and materialism.

Most thinkers who affirm life after death, or at least its possibility, accept ontological dualism, enunciated paradigmatically by Descartes. This Cartesian dualism involves two distinguishable theses. First, contrary to identism, the mind is one thing, the brain is another thing. This is the *numerical* thesis, stating that the mind and the brain are numerically distinct.

Second, the mind is composed of one kind of stuff whereas the brain is composed of another kind of stuff. This is the *ontological* thesis, stating that the mind and the brain are ontologically different *kinds* of things. The essential difference is that the mind is an experiencing thing whereas the brain is comprised of nonexperiencing things. Brain cells (neurons), along with the entities of which they are composed, are assumed to be wholly devoid of experience.

The problems created by this ontological dualism led to the collapse of dualism into materialistic identism. The basic problem is how mind and brain, being utterly different in kind, could interact.

How could a mental or spiritual being influence bits of insentient matter? And how could bits of matter, which, like billiard balls, influence each other by colliding with each other, influence a purely spiritual entity, which does not have the property of impenetrability?

Descartes' followers, such as Malebranche and Geulincx, solved the problem by appealing to God. Fully conceding that mind and body could not interact, they said that God coordinated their behavior, making them *appear* to interact. Some such appeal was made by all dualists at the time, including Descartes himself.[33] As William James said, "For thinkers of that age, 'God' was the great solvent of all absurdities."[34]

The contemporary form of dualism's mind-body problem is the question of how the mind, with its experience, could have emerged in the evolutionary process out of a brain composed of wholly nonexperiencing entities. A few contemporary dualists continued the appeal to a supernatural deity to solve this mystery. Richard Swinburne, for example, said:

> [S]cience cannot explain the evolution of a mental life. That is to say, . . . there is nothing in the nature of certain physical events . . . to give rise to connections to [mental events]. . . . God, being omnipotent, would have the power to produce a soul.[35]

Most contemporary dualists reject this appeal to a *deus ex machina*, but this rejection leaves them with an insoluble mystery, as some of them have admitted. Geoffrey Madell, for example, said that "the appearance of consciousness in the course of evolution must appear for the dualist to be an utterly inexplicable emergence." With regard to the more general problem of interaction, Madell admitted that "the nature of the causal connection between the mental and the physical, as the Cartesian conceives of it, is utterly mysterious."[36]

Materialists have used this problem of dualistic interaction to reject dualism in favor of materialistic identism. In rejecting the

idea that the mind and brain are two things, materialism rejects not
only the ontological thesis, according to which mind and body are
composed of different kinds of stuff, but also the numerical thesis,
according to which they are different entities. Materialists hence do
not have to answer the question of how mind and brain, being different in kind, can interact.

The assumption that this would solve the mind-body problem,
however, turned out to be an illusion. There is still the problem of how
experience could emerge from a brain composed of nonexperiencing
entities, as some materialists have admitted. Colin McGinn, for
example, asked: "How could the aggregation of millions of individually
insentient neurons generate subjective awareness?"[37]

> [W]e do not know how consciousness might have arisen by
> natural processes from antecedently existing material things.
> Somehow or other sentience sprang from pulpy matter, giving
> matter an inner aspect, but we have no idea how this leap
> was propelled.

McGinn's reference to *natural* processes here was essential to his point.
"One is tempted," he added,

> to turn to divine assistance: for only a kind of miracle could
> produce *this* from *that*. It would take a supernatural magician
> to extract consciousness from matter. Consciousness appears
> to introduce a sharp break in the natural order—a point at
> which scientific naturalism runs out of steam.[38]

McGinn admitted, in other words, that materialism, which necessarily
eschews any appeal to supernaturalism, cannot solve the mind-body
problem. McGinn said, in fact, that the mind-body relation should
be classified not as a *problem*, which might be solved some day, but
as a *mystery*, because it is insoluble in principle.[39]

The problem of how experience emerges out of the brain is not,
moreover, the only part of the mind-body problem that materialism
cannot solve. It also cannot explain "mental causation"—namely, how

experience, with its purposes, can act back upon the brain. Although this is something we presuppose all the time — as when we pick up a glass of water *because* we want a drink — materialists have admitted that they cannot explain it. For example, Jaegwon Kim, after working on this problem for almost twenty years, said that materialism seems "to be up against a dead end."[40]

Closely related to this issue of mental causation is another question that materialists cannot answer, which is how we can act with a degree of freedom. Even materialists admit that we inevitably presuppose that we do. John Searle, for example, pointed out that "we can't act otherwise than on the assumption of freedom, no matter how much we learn about how the world works as a determined physical system."[41]

Searle's materialistic worldview, however, led him to say that "since everything can be accounted for in terms of . . . particles and their relations, there is simply no room for freedom of the will." Accordingly, having said that "I would like to be able to keep both my commonsense conceptions and my scientific beliefs," Searle added that "when it comes to the question of freedom and determinism, I am . . . unable to reconcile the two."[42]

Ironically, although materialism was initially accepted to avoid dualism's mind-body problem, it ended up being even less adequate than dualism to the facts that we all presuppose. Dualists, affirming a numerical distinction between the mind and the brain, could at least affirm human freedom. That is, by regarding the mind as a distinct actuality with the power of self-determination, dualists could explain our assumption that we make free decisions. But materialists, seeing the mind as numerically identical with the brain, cannot regard it as a unified agent with the power of self-determination. The impossibility of thinking of the brain as a self-determining organism has been brought out by Daniel Dennett's description of it as consisting of billions of "miniagents and microagents (with no single Boss)."[43]

This superiority of dualism to materialism is limited, however, because dualists cannot explain how the mind's freely made decisions can affect the brain and hence the rest of the body. They cannot, therefore, explain the freedom of our bodily action, including our speaking.[44]

Given this account of the mind-body problem, we can see why life after death is widely ruled out by intellectuals who reject supernaturalist explanations. Although dualism is compatible with—and has in fact been widely associated with—belief in the "immortality of the soul," dualism requires supernaturalism to explain the very existence of the mind and its interaction with its body. There is wide agreement, therefore, that a naturalistic worldview must be monistic in the sense of affirming that all *actual* entities—meaning entities that can act and be acted upon—are of the same ontological type.

It is this connection between naturalism and (pluralistic) monism that explains the preference of the scientific and philosophical communities for materialism over dualism. Even if the materialistic version of pluralistic monism is more inadequate than dualism, the thought persists, and rightly so, that a solution will be possible only on a (pluralistic) monistic basis. But as long as this preference for monism translates into an acceptance of materialism, belief in life after death, and hence salvation₂, will be a very minority position except in supernaturalistic circles.

PANEXPERIENTIALISM MAKES LIFE AFTER DEATH CONCEIVABLE

This situation could change, however, if another kind of pluralistic monism became widely accepted, one that embodies the strength of dualism, which is the numerical distinction between mind and brain. Such a position would involve—contrary to the widespread assumption that interaction entails ontological dualism—a *nondualistic interactionism*. This is precisely the kind of position offered by Whitehead's process philosophy.

The reason Whiteheadian philosophy can combine interactionism with pluralistic monism is that it rejects the Cartesian assumption common to both dualism and materialism, namely, that the physical world is composed of what Whitehead called "vacuous actualities"—meaning things that are fully actual and yet devoid of experience.[45] Whitehead affirmed, instead, a position that can be called "panexperientialism," according to which experience goes all the way down, to the most elementary units of nature. Although this position is still widely assumed to be too absurd to be taken seriously, I have argued at length elsewhere that all the standard objections can be overcome.[46]

One example is the fact that panexperientialism—usually under the older name "panpsychism"—is commonly rejected on the grounds that it implies that things such as sticks and stones have consciousness, or at least experience of some sort, in spite of showing no signs of spontaneity, which is surely the best indicator of a unified experience. Although this criticism is valid against one type of panexperientialism, it does not apply to the Whiteheadian-Hartshornean type, which distinguishes between genuine individuals, which have a unified experience, and aggregational societies of individuals (such as rocks, stars, and computers), which do not. To emphasize this point, I speak not simply of panexperientialism but of "panexperientialism with organizational duality."[47]

Genuine individuals include not only simple individuals, meaning the most elementary units of nature, but also what Hartshorne has called "compound individuals," in which more or less complex individuals are compounded out of simpler ones. Every compound individual has a dominant member, which gives the entity as a whole a unity of both experience and self-determining agency. In humans, this dominant member is called the mind, psyche, or soul.

Given this view, according to which the mind is numerically distinct from the brain, the idea that it survives apart from the brain is at least ontologically possible. Even Hartshorne admitted this.[48] The question of whether the soul does in fact survive should, as Whitehead himself suggested, "be decided on more special evidence, religious or otherwise, provided that it is trustworthy."[49]

Whitehead was probably thinking of not only reported events associated with religions, such as the post-crucifixion appearances of Jesus, but also of the evidence from psychical research (now usually called "parapsychology"). Whitehead, after all, was at Cambridge University with Henry Sidgwick, the first president of the Society for Psychical Research, and he was heavily influenced by the writings of William James, the intellectual leader of the American Society for Psychical Research.

At that time, the evidence for life after death studied by psychical researchers—evidence from apparitions, mediumistic messages, out-of-body experiences, and cases suggestive of possession and reincarnation—was highly ambiguous. But a few years ago, I studied the evidence that is now available and found that it is quite strong. My own conclusion was, in fact, that today the best empirical evidence, if approached in the light of a worldview that makes it possible, supports the belief that our conscious lives do continue after bodily death.

Given the Whiteheadian version of naturalism, therefore, life after death does not require supernaturalism. But the fact that supernatural intervention is unnecessary does not imply the unimportance of divine influence. If the human soul now has the natural capacity to survive bodily death, it has this capacity only because of billions of years of previous divine activity. Also, even if the soul now has the capacity to survive the death of its bodily organism, it would actually do so only because it is continually receiving fresh divine aims from God.

To express this point, John Cobb has spoken of the "resurrection of the soul," a phrase that combines the points made by each of the two traditional phrases. Like "immortality of the soul," it implies that the power to survive death is now inherent in the soul, so that no supernatural intervention is needed. But like "resurrection of the body," it points to the idea that this power is not *simply* inherent, but was and still is dependent on divine influence.[50] From this perspective, it is of interest that New Testament scholar Gregory Riley has argued that the earliest Christians spoke of the "resurrection of the soul" instead of "resurrection of the body."[51]

Process theologians can, in any case, think in terms of salvation as the sanctification of the soul within the framework of a fully naturalistic theism, according to which divine influence is by persuasion alone. This divine *modus operandi* creates saints within the span of an earthly life only occasionally. However, given a return to the medieval view, according to which the divine persuasion works on us during a lengthy process of purgation and sanctification after bodily death, hope for universal salvation$_2$ is intelligible.

3 Salvation$_3$

The third dimension of the salvation proclaimed in the message of Jesus involved a coming time in which God's will would be "done on earth." This new era would be one in which the present order, which is now ruled by demonic values, would be replaced by a religious-social-political-economic order based on divine values — such as truth, compassion, and justice — with everyone having their "daily bread." Salvation in this sense was at the center of the "social gospel" as articulated by Walter Rauschenbusch, who contrasted the "kingdom of God" with the "kingdom of evil."[52]

The neo-orthodox movement, led in America by Reinhold Niebuhr, rejected the contention that Christian faith should be reoriented around a reign of God on earth. But today, through various forms of political and liberation theology, this emphasis has returned, but with a difference. Today, surely at least partly in response to the growing awareness of the reality and nature of the American empire, theologians and Jesus scholars are increasingly pointing out that demonic power for Jesus and the New Testament more generally, especially its final book, was embodied in the Roman empire. The gospel of Jesus was, therefore, an "anti-imperial gospel."[53]

This reorientation of the Christian gospel around Jesus' message of the reign of God has been affirmed by process theologians. John Cobb, describing the teaching of Jesus as "contra-imperial," wrote that "the clearest and most accurate way of presenting Jesus' contra-imperial vision is by focusing on his teaching about . . . the *Basileia theou*." Cobb added:

> The threat of U.S. imperial rule over the whole world must certainly be addressed more directly in faithfulness to Jesus. . . . . We who call ourselves Christians are called to fan the sparks of [Jesus'] message into a flame that can help to reverse the headlong plunge of our nation into the lust for world domination.[54]

Whitehead wrote that religion at its best aims at making "the common life the City of God that it should be" and that "[t]he great social ideal for religion is that it should be the common basis for the unity of civilization."[55] I have suggested a way to work toward that end. The basic question is whether there is a possible political order for the world in which divine values—such as the Golden Rule, which is enshrined in virtually all religious traditions--could become the basis for policy.

I then suggest that this question amounts to asking: What political structure might allow decisions to be made that would approximate those of an ideal observer—a being characterized by omniscience as well as universal benevolence based on compassion for all?[56]

The answer, I propose, is global democracy, based on a global bill of rights, in which the interests of all peoples are truly and equally represented. With the emergence of such a democratic government at the global level, we could protect human rights in all countries, address the global ecological crisis, overcome global apartheid, and eliminate the war-system with its inevitable imperialism and terrorism. On this basis, I conclude that we Christians "need to live out the implications of our fidelity to the God of Jesus by participating fully in a worldwide movement to democratize human civilization."[57]

Accordingly, if the present demonic rule of the planet is replaced by a rule based on divine values through the creation of global democracy, this development, like all previous advances in evolution and in human history, will be a victory for divine persuasion.

4 Salvation₄

The fourth dimension of the salvation preached by Jesus was a reign of God in the individual heart and in social relations, which in the message of Jesus was made possible by faith in the first three dimensions of salvation. Much modern liberal theology has been deficient here due to its inability to affirm the second and third dimensions and in some cases even the first dimension. But process theology, as we have seen, can affirm all three. It can thereby provide a strong basis for individuals, churches, and movements to orient their lives fully around the divine battle against demonic forces — those forces both in the human heart and society.

Winning the battle against demonic forces in the human heart can, of course, be extremely complex and difficult. But belief in the first three types of salvation can go far in the direction.

Winning the battle in society at every level, including humanity as a whole, will be, if anything, even more complex and difficult. But essential to this task, I have suggested, will be the effort to institutionalize democracy at the global level.

This effort would be opposed mightily by the plutocratic and imperialistic forces that are now in control. This effort will, accordingly, require courage comparable to that of those early Christians whose resistance to the empire of that age led them to martyrdom. Conservative Christians, when they see that their Christian identity requires them to oppose the empire of our time, already have an eschatology that can support the needed courage. Process theology, I am suggesting, can provide such an eschatology for liberal Christians.

Notes

1. Austin Farrer, *Faith and Speculation: An Essay in Philosophical Theology* (New York University Press, 1967), 170.

2   Alfred North Whitehead, *Process and Reality*, corrected edition, ed. David Ray Griffin and Donald W. Sherburne (The Free Press, 1978), 340.

3   Ibid., 347.

4   Ibid., 346.

5   Ibid., 340.

6   Ibid., 347.

7   Charles Hartshorne, *The Logic of Perfection and Other Essays in Neoclassical Metaphysics* (Open Court. 1962), 132.

8   Hartshorne, *Omnipotence and Other Theological Mistakes* (State University of New York Press, 1984), 110.

9   Ibid., 4. Although Hartshorne in this passage seemed to deny life ("a career") after bodily death altogether, I inserted "infinite career" because it is only that which he denied when writing carefully, as shown in passages in which he rejected "infinite careers" after death (47, 48, 117), careers with "temporally infinite futures" (36), careers that go on "forever" (40).

10 Ibid., 117.

11 Schubert M. Ogden, *The Reality of God and Other Essays* (Harper & Row, 1966), Ch. 8, "The Promise of Faith," 206–30, at 229–30.

12 Schubert M. Ogden, "The Meaning of Christian Hope," *Union Seminary Quarterly Review* 30 (Winter-Summer 1975), 161.

13 Edward Henderson, "Austin Farrer and Process Theology: Notes on 'The Prior Actuality of God'" (unpublished ms., 12).

14 John B. Cobb, Jr., "The Resurrection of the Soul," *Harvard Theological Review* 80/2 (1987), 213–27.

15 Marjorie Hewitt Suchocki, *The End of Evil: Process Eschatology in Historical Context* (State University of New York Press, 1988), 165, summarizing the argument of her article "The Question of

Immortality," *Journal of Religion* 57/3 (July 1977): 288–306, in which she responded to Ogden's "The Meaning of Christian Hope."

16 Suchocki, *God, Christ, Church: A Practical Guide to Process Theology*, new revised edition (Crossroad, 1989),198.

17 David Ray Griffin, *Reenchantment without Supernaturalism: A Process Philosophy of Religion* (Cornell University Press, 2001), 230–36.

18 Suchocki, *The End of Evil*, 90–91.

19 Suchocki, *God, Christ, Church*, 207.

20 Ibid., 207.

21 Suchocki, *The End of Evil*, 94.

22 In two passages quoted by Suchocki (*The End of Evil*, 92), White-head suggested that "immediacy"—which Suchocki took to refer to *subjective* immediacy—is retained in God (*Process and Reality*, 346, 351). And Hartshorne held, as she pointed out, that "God prehends the fullness of the satisfaction" and hence "retains the immediacy of the satisfaction" (*The End of Evil*, 166 n. 2, referring to Hartshorne's contribution to "Three Responses to Neville's *Creativity and God*," *Process Studies* 10/3-4 [Fall-Winter 1980]: 93–97).

23 Suchocki, *The End of Evil*, 102.

24 Suchocki, *God, Christ, Church*, 211.

25 Ibid., 210–216; *The End of Evil*, 105–14.

26 David Ray Griffin, "Review of Marjorie Suchocki's *The End of Evil*," *Process Studies* 18/1 (Spring 1989), 57–62.

27 Suchocki, *God, Christ, Church*, 206, 208.

28 Bruce R. Reichenbach has pointed out that for those who accept a deity with omnipotence in the traditional sense, materialism provides no obstacle to belief in life after bodily death. See Reichenbach, *Is Man the Phoenix? A Study of Immortality* (Christian University Press, 1978), 84–85.

29 Alfred North Whitehead, *Religion in the Making* (1926; reprint by Fordham University Press, 1996), 111.

30 Whitehead, *Essays in Science and Philosophy* (Philosophical Library,

1947), 116.

31   J. M. E. McTaggart, *Some Dogmas of Religion* (Edward Arnold, 1906), 105.

32   Whitehead, *Adventures of Ideas* (The Free Press, 1967), 208.

33   Gordon Baker and Katherine J. Morris, *Descartes' Dualism* (Routledge, 1996), 153–54, 167–70. On Malebranche and Geulincx, see F. C. Copleston, *A History of Philosophy*, vol. 4: *Descartes to Leibniz* (Burns Oates, 1960), 117–19, 188–90.

34   William James, *Some Problems of Philosophy* (Longman & Green, 1911), 194.

35   Richard Swinburne, *The Evolution of the Soul* (Clarendon, 1986), 198–99. Swinburne is a dualist, but he rightly says that this problem is the same whether one is a dualist or a materialist.

36   Geoffrey Madell, *Mind and Materialism* (The University Press, 1988), 2, 140–41.

37   Colin McGinn, *The Problem of Consciousness: Essays Toward a Resolution* (Basil Blackwell, 1991), 1.

38   Ibid., 45.

39   Ibid., 29.

40   Jaegwon Kim, *Supervenience and Mind: Selected Philosophical Essays* (Cambridge University Press, 1993), 367.

41   John R. Searle, *Minds, Brains, and Science: The 1984 Reith Lectures* (British Broadcasting Corporation, 1984), 97.

42   Ibid., 86.

43   Daniel Dennett, *Consciousness Explained* (Little, Brown, 1991), 458.

44. I have discussed the problems of both dualism and materialism in David Ray Griffin, *Unsnarling the World-Knot: Consciousness, Freedom, and the Mind-Body Problem* (University of California Press, 1998), Chapter 6.

45   Whitehead, *Process and Reality*, 29, 167.

46   Griffin, *Unsnarling the World Knot*, Ch. 7. Briefer treatments can be found in my *Religion and Scientific Naturalism: Overcoming the Conflicts*, Ch. 6, and "Panexperientialist Physicalism and the Mind-Body

Problem," *Journal of Consciousness Studies* 4/3 (1997), 248–68.

47 Griffin, *Reenchantment without Supernaturalism*, 6.

48 Hartshorne's metaphysical argument against subjective immortality was based on the idea that "[i]mmortality is a divine trait" (*Creative Synthesis and Philosophic Method* [Open Court, 1970], 289). He believed, therefore, that it would be unreasonable to think of ourselves as having "temporally infinite futures" (1984: 36). Hartshorne did *not* argue that the mind-body relation is such that life after death is impossible. Accordingly, as Donald Wayne Viney has pointed out (*Charles Hartshorne and the Existence of God* [State University of New York Press, 1985], 116), Hartshorne's personal rejection of life after death does not mean that his philosophical position makes it impossible. Hartshorne, in fact, granted this in a 1994 letter to me, which is available at the Center for Process Studies.

49 Whitehead, *Religion in the Making*, 111.

50 John B. Cobb, Jr., "The Resurrection of the Soul," *Harvard Theological Review* 80/2 (1987), 213–27.

51 Gregory Riley, *Resurrection Reconsidered: Thomas and John in Controversy* (Fortress, 1995).

52 Walter Rauschenbusch, *A Theology for the Social Gospel* (1917; Abington, 1945).

53 This phrase is used in Richard A. Horsley, *Jesus and Empire: The Kingdom of God and the New World Disorder* (Fortress, 2003), 13. See also Richard A. Horsley and Neil Asher Silberman, *The Message and the Kingdom: How Jesus and Paul Ignited a Revolution and Transformed the Ancient World* (Grosset/Putnam, 1997), and Klaus Wengst, *Pax Romana and the Peace of Jesus Christ* (Fortress, 1987).

54 John B. Cobb, Jr., "Commonwealth & Empire," in David Ray Griffin, John B. Cobb Jr., Richard Falk, and Catherine Keller, *The American Empire and the Commonwealth of God: A Political, Economic, Religious Statement* (Westminster John Knox Press, 2006).

55 Whitehead, *Religion in the Making*, 39; Whitehead, *Adventures of Ideas*, 171.

56 I am one of many thinkers who hold that the best definition of the "right" and the "good" is "what an ideal observer would prefer." See,

for example, Charles Taliaferro, "Relativising the Ideal Observer Theory," *Philosophy and Phenomenological Research* 49/1 (1988): 123–38; Roderick Firth, "Ethical Absolutism and the Ideal Observer," *Philosophy and Phenomenological Research* 12 (1952): 317–45; and Charles Reynolds, "A Proposal for Understanding the Place of Reason in Christian Ethics," *Journal of Religion* 50/2 (April 1970): 155–68.

57   David Ray Griffin, "Global Democracy: Precondition for a World Based on Divine Values," unpublished manuscript. Some of the ideas in this manuscript have been published in "The Moral Need for Global Democracy," in *Belonging Together: Faith and Politics in a Relational World*, ed. Douglas Sturm (P&F Press, 2003), 119–39, and "Global Imperialism or Global Democracy: The Present Alternatives," in Griffin et al., *The American Empire and the Commonwealth of God*.

CHAPTER SIX

Process Theodicy and Climate Change

GIVEN THE TRADITIONAL DOCTRINE OF DIVINE OMNIPOTENCE (combined with divine goodness), the most serious problem for theodicy today is: Why would God bring us—or allow us to be brought—to a point at which the very survival of civilization is threatened?

This threat is now widely discussed in environmental and scientific circles. For example:

- Canadian lawyer, Minister of Parliament, and former seminarian Elizabeth May gave a lecture entitled "Can Civilization Survive Climate Change?"[1]

- *New Yorker* writer Elizabeth Kolbert wrote: "It may seem impossible to imagine that a technologically advanced society could choose, in essence, to destroy itself, but that is what we are now in the process of doing."[2]

- Lester Brown, who founded the institute that publishes the annual *State of the World* books, wrote: "[W]e have a new challenge: to save civilization itself."[3]

- A statement by 20 scientists who had won the Blue Planet Prize said: "In the face of an absolutely unprecedented emergency, society [must] take dramatic action to avert a collapse of civilization."[4]

- Noam Chomsky wrote that "we are moving toward what may in fact be the ultimate genocide—the destruction of the environment."[5]

A test for a theodicy today is whether it makes people complacent in the face of this crisis. The traditional doctrine of divine omnipotence, argued Jewish theologian Richard Rubenstein in *After Auschwitz*, means that whatever happens must ultimately be in harmony with the divine will. Therefore, he said, no Jew—and, by implication, no morally sensitive person—should believe in the God who determines the course of history. Black theologian William R. Jones made a similar argument in *Is God a White Racist?* The traditional doctrine of divine omnipotence, both Rubenstein and Jones argued, tends to create acceptance and complacency in the face of horrendous evil.[6]

If so, there is an analogous problem with global warming and the climate change it causes.

1 Supernaturalism and Climate Complacency

The traditional doctrine of omnipotence can be considered the central tenet of *supernaturalism*, according to which what we call the natural world, including human beings, is under the control, at least potentially, of a divine being. This view is exemplified in Evangelical theologian Millard Erickson, who says he "operates with a definite supernaturalism—God resides outside the world and intervenes periodically within the natural processes through miracles."[7] Nature, Erickson says, "is under God's control; and while it ordinarily functions in uniform and predictable ways in obedience to the laws he has structured into it, he can and does also act within it in ways which contravene these normal patterns (miracles)."[8]

This doctrine tends to promote climate complacency. The United States takes threats from climate change less seriously, polls indicate, than any of the other industrialized countries.[9] It seems probable that there is a causal connection between these polls and the fact, according to a 2012 Gallup poll, that 46 per cent of Americans believe that our world was created within the past 10,000 years.[10] These people reject, in other words, the evolutionary view, according to which the present state of our world was formed through a several-billion-year process.

Insofar as people accept some form of theism, according to which our world was created by a divine power, the evolutionary view suggests, or at least is consistent with, the idea that the divine power is not omnipotence — not the power to bring about effects unilaterally. By contrast, the idea that our world was created only a few thousand years ago entails that kind of omnipotence, according to which the divine power — henceforth simply called "God" — brought about our world unilaterally. And if God has this kind of power, then God would be able to prevent (unilaterally) any and every type of evil. Accordingly, if God does not want the world to be destroyed by either nuclear war or global warming, then the world will not be destroyed. This view, which is accepted by most Evangelical Christians, encourages climate complacency, which goes far to explain why self-identified Evangelicals are, as polls have consistently shown, less likely than Americans in general to be very concerned about global warming.[11]

U.S. POLITICIANS

Besides informing the worldview of a large number of ordinary Americans, this supernaturalism influences the thinking of many U.S. political leaders, including their thinking about climate change. Take, for example, Senator James Inhofe, who in 2012 published a book called *The Greatest Hoax*. In this book, Inhofe cited Genesis 8:22 — "As long as the earth remains there will be seedtime and harvest, cold and heat, winter and summer, day and night" — and quoted a preacher who, speaking on a bitterly cold morning, said that "more than 3,000 years ago God promised that cold and heat should not cease, so I am strengthened by this weather which emphasizes the sureness of His promises." According to Inhofe, "This is what a lot of alarmists forget. God is still up there, and He promised to maintain the seasons."[12] It is arrogant, said Inhofe, to "think that we, human beings, would be able to change what He is doing in the climate."

Referring to the same passage, U.S. Congressman John Shimkus said: "I believe that's the infallible word of God, and that's the way it's going to be for his creation. . . . The Earth will end only when God declares it's time to be over."[14]

Taking issue with Secretary of State John Kerry's statement that climate change is "a challenge to our responsibilities as the guardians . . . of God's creation," highly influential talk-show host Rush Limbaugh said: "If you believe in God, then intellectually you cannot believe in manmade global warming." Kerry's statement, Limbaugh complained, implied that "we are so . . . omnipotent that we can . . . destroy the climate."[15]

END-TIMERS AND EXTREME WEATHER

One of the central doctrines of this kind of Christian faith is the traditional belief in "the Second Coming of Jesus Christ," according to which Jesus will return at the end of the world. A 2013 article published in the *Political Research Quarterly* found that "believers in Christian end-times theology are less likely to support policies designed to curb global warming than are other Americans." Whereas it makes sense that most other Americans "would support preserving the Earth for future generations," said this article, the "end-times believers would rationally perceive such efforts to be ultimately futile, and hence ill-advised."[16]

The type of climate change that has most gotten the attention of Americans is extreme weather—such as hurricanes, flooding, and deadly heat and drought—which has become noticeably worse in recent years. End-times believers generally think of extreme-weather events as "acts of God." When end-times preacher John Hagee, who heads a megachurch in San Antonio,[17] was asked whether he believed Hurricane Katrina to be divine punishment for immorality, he replied:

> All hurricanes are acts of God, because God controls the heavens. I believe that New Orleans had a level of sin that was offensive to God. . . . [T]here was to be a homosexual parade there on the Monday that the Katrina came. . . . And I believe that the Hurricane Katrina was, in fact, the judgment of God against the city of New Orleans."[18]

Likewise, David Crowe, the executive director of Restore America, also spoke to the question of why Hurricane Katrina occurred. "The answer," he explained, "is found in understanding that man is not in control. God is! Everything in the sky, the sea and on earth is subject to His control."[19]

EVANGELICAL ENVIRONMENTALISM?

For a brief time, it appeared that much of the Evangelical world would form an alliance with the environmental community. But in 2011, Molly Redden, writing in the *New Republic*, asked "Whatever Happened to the Evangelical-Environmental Alliance?" She answered: "Creationism and a 'God is in charge' belief became prominent again, along with a sense that any attempt to take climate change seriously was somehow unfaithful."[20]

How did this idea of divine power become standard Christian thinking? The answer involves the idea of creation out of nothing.

2 Creation out of Nothing, Creation out of Chaos

Many people think the idea of divine omnipotence is biblical. And that is true, if "omnipotence" means that God is the *supreme power* in reality, the power to bring our world into existence. But to theologians such as Calvinist Millard Erickson, that is not enough. Rather, he endorses Calvin's view, according which God is called "omnipotent" because "he regulates all things according to his secret plan, which depends solely upon itself."[21]

Calvin on this point did not disagree with Martin Luther, who, denying that God simply foreknows (without determining) future events, says that God "does all things according to His own immutable, eternal and infallible will."[22] Nor did either Calvin or Martin Luther disagree with St. Augustine, who said that even those wills that "follow the world are so entirely at the disposal of God, that He turns them whithersoever He wills, and whensoever He wills," which means that God "does in the hearts of even wicked men whatsoever He wills."[23]

Why did these theologians say that God has the power to *fully* control everything in the world—both "nature" as the term is now usually understood, and human wills, which are generally thought to have a degree of freedom? Erickson explained:

> God did not work with something which was in existence. He brought into existence the very raw material which he employed. If this were not the case, God would . . . have been limited by having to work with the intrinsic characteristics of the raw material which he employed.[24]

Erickson has thereby provided a clear statement of the traditional doctrine of *creatio ex nihilo*, meaning "creation out of absolutely nothing." But why did Erickson endorse that doctrine? We can answer this by saying that he got it from Calvin, who got it from Luther, who got it from Augustine. But that just pushes the question back: Why did these theologians believe this? The standard answer is that Augustine and other early theologians got it from the Bible. But good evidence has been provided that this is not so.

JON LEVENSON ON OMNIPOTENCE AND CREATION

It is widely thought that the doctrine of *creatio ex nihilo* was expressed by the first verses of *Genesis*, translated as: "In the beginning God created the heaven and the earth." But in a book entitled *Creation and the Persistence of Evil: The Jewish Drama of Divine Omnipotence*, Jon Levenson, a professor of Jewish Studies at Harvard University, argued against this view. If "properly understood," says Levenson, Genesis 1:1–2:3 "cannot be invoked in support of the developed Jewish, Christian, and Muslim doctrine of *creatio ex nihilo*."[25]

Part of his argument was that this passage is more correctly trans-lated, "When God began to create the heaven and the earth," with the second verse stating that the world was a formless void.[26] That this is the preferred reading is now commonplace. But this means that the Bible's opening passage supports the doctrine of creation out of chaos, not out of nothing. Levenson also supports the argument of his book, the title of which speaks of "the persistence of evil," with other parts of the Hebrew Bible showing that in creating the world, the chaos was only circumscribed, not annihilated.[27]

GERHARD MAY'S *CREATIO EX NIHILO*

In response, one could argue that, even if Levenson's view is correct, the doctrine of *creatio ex nihilo* can still be considered biblical by Christians. This argument could be formulated in terms of four points:

1. There are passages in the New Testament — such as John 1:3, Romans 4:17, Colossians 1:16, and Hebrews 11:3 — that provide evidence that the doctrine of *creatio ex nihilo* was held by first-century Christians.

2. While these passages admittedly do not in themselves unam-biguously reflect this doctrine, they are consistent with it.

3. The doctrine is unambiguously reflected in inter-testamental Judaism, so "primitive Christianity found the doctrine ready-made in the Jewish tradition."

4. Therefore, the New Testament passages in question can be assumed to have presupposed the doctrine of *creatio ex nihilo*.

German theologian Gerhard May formulated this argument in his book, *The Doctrine of "Creation out of Nothing" in Early Christian Thought*—but only to undermine it, arguing that neither these nor any other New Testament passages provide evidence for this doctrine.[28]

May made this historical argument, even though he, *qua* theologian, accepted the doctrine, believing that it was rightly seen to be necessary to protect the biblical view of divine power, once Christian theologians were exposed to the Greek idea that our world was formed by the creator out of some pre-existent stuff.[29] This exposure was, more specifically, to Middle Platonism, which said, like the Hebrew Scriptures, that the *ordered* cosmos originated in time, but that there are "three principles"—not only God but also Ideas and Matter—that are co-eternal.[30]

May argued that there was an "inner necessity" for Christian thinkers to reject this doctrine in favor of *creatio ex nihilo*.[31] But May's claim is contradicted by his own account.

First, after being exposed to Greek philosophy, Jewish theologians had felt no such inner necessity. Hellenistic Judaism in general and Philo in particular, May pointed out, saw no contradiction between the biblical doctrine of God's power and "the acceptance of a matter that had not originated in time." May reported, furthermore, that *creatio ex nihilo* was not accepted by Jewish thinkers until the Middle Ages. Accordingly, May was able to base his contention—that the Platonic view contradicts the true biblical view—only on the question-begging claim that these Jewish thinkers were insufficiently critical.[32]

Second, although May suggested that Christian thinkers had reason to be more critical, he points out that many second-century theologians considered "orthodox" by later standards, including Justin Martyr, Athenagoras, and Clement of Alexandria, held that the "acceptance of an unformed matter was entirely reconcilable with biblical monotheism." Justin even argued that Plato "took over the doctrine that God made the cosmos out of unoriginate matter from the opening verses of Genesis."[33]

Third, although May contended that when Christian theologians finally developed the doctrine of *creatio ex nihilo*, they did so "partly to express opposition" to Middle Platonism, one would expect such opposition to have been expressed from the outset. May's account shows, instead, that when some Christian theologians began rejecting the idea of creation out of chaos in the latter part of the second century, they did so because of the threat raised by Marcion's version of gnosticism.[34]

Besides accepting the eternity of matter, Marcion regarded it as *evil*. Our world is filled with evil, argued Marcion, because it was formed out of evil matter by the Hebrew Bible's creator-God, who is different from the supreme God revealed in Jesus. Marcion thereby contradicted not only the monotheism of Christian faith but its conviction that the world is essentially good, only contingently evil. As May points out, it was because of Marcion that the church started rejecting, as heretical, the idea that our world was created out of unformed matter.[35] In support of this conclusion, May said:

> Marcion's teaching that matter and the world created from it were bad and hateful could only make it obvious in an impressive way what dangerous dualistic consequences could develop from the philosophical doctrine of the pre-existence of matter.

But to say that such dangerous consequences *could develop* is very different from saying that the Middle Platonic notion of "three principles" *necessarily* implied such consequences.

In fact, May himself pointed out that most philosophers who affirmed the existence of uncreated matter defined it as being "without qualities." It, therefore, could not coherently be said to be essentially either good *or* evil, so Marcion's idea of matter as essentially evil was, far from being a logical implication from the idea of formless matter, an *incoherent addition* to it. Thanks to Marcion, nevertheless, the idea of uncreated matter became subject to guilt by association, with the result that Christian theologians began attacking the idea of uncreated matter as such.[36]

HERMOGENES: LOST OPPORTUNITY

A fourth way in which May contradicted his claim about the necessity of *creatio ex nihilo* involves his discussion of Hermogenes, the theologian who was the primary victim of the anti-Marcionite development. There was, May's own account indicates, nothing inherently objectionable about the theology of Hermogenes. He was "emphatically anxious to ensure the absolute goodness of the creator God." In employing the idea of unoriginate matter, his primary concern was to explain the origin of evil in a way that protected that absolute goodness. Although Hermogenes' own writings are no longer extant, his basic idea seems to be that "the ground of the evil present in the world" is "the trace of the original disorder of matter remaining in every created thing."

If, by contrast, we supposed God to have created our world out of nothing, we could have no coherent explanation of the origin of evil, "because as perfect Goodness [God] could only have created good." According to Hermogenes, therefore, the idea of *creatio ex nihilo*, by saying that God is the source of literally everything—including evil—would threaten the perfect goodness of God.[37]

Besides supporting creation out of chaos to protect the absolute goodness of the Creator, Hermogenes's theology should not have been considered heretical. In arguing that Genesis 1:2 supported creation out of chaos, Hermogenes was following, May pointed out, "a widespread expository tradition." Also, far from regarding matter itself as evil, Hermogenes pointed out that "matter before its ordering is without qualities" and therefore "neither good nor evil." Therefore, Hermogenes stood firmly against Manichean, Marcionite dualism.[38]

Nevertheless, May said, "When Hermogenes put forward his ideas, literary polemic against him seems to have begun almost immediately," because of the context:

> In the last decades of the second century the process by which the Catholic Church fenced itself off from the gnostic heretics was in full swing, and with it there was a critical reaction

against philosophical reinterpretations of Christian doctrine and especially against all forms of intellectual syncretism. In this historical situation a synthesis of Christianity and Platonism, such as Hermogenes was attempting, could no longer be pursued; to undertake it was, in the atmosphere of anti-gnostic theology, immediately to incur the verdict of heresy.[39]

A fifth reason provided by May against his own claim was his suggestions that *creatio ex nihilo* had been originated by theologians less philosophically able than Hermogenes. The earliest opponent of Hermogenes, Theophilus of Antioch, was "the first church theologian known to us," said May, "to use unambiguously the substance and the terminology of the doctrine of *creatio ex nihilo*." This doctrine, which removes all restrictions on God's creative activity by declaring "the free decision of God's will [to be] the sole ground of creation," acknowledged May, was bound to make the biblical concept of God "a philosophical problem." However, he added, "this is a question far beyond Theophilus."[40]

Theophilus's polemic on this issue then influenced Hippolytus, Tertullian, and probably Irenaeus, the other founder, along with Theophilus himself, "of the church doctrine of *creatio ex nihilo*." Irenaeus rejected the Platonic view that God can only will "the best possible" in favor of "the absolute freedom and omnipotence of the biblical God," which "must rule and dominate in everything" so that "everything else must give way to it." However, May acknowledged, "Beyond the demands of the controversy with gnosticism, cosmological questions scarcely worried Irenaeus," whose position was "only attainable because Irenaeus is quite unaware of philosophical problems."[41]

In any case, the rejection of creation out of chaos, which had been the understanding of the biblical tradition for over a millennium, occurred very suddenly: "For Tertullian and Hippolytus [and also Origen] it is already the fixed Christian position that God created the world out of absolutely nothing."[42]

Apart from the battle occasioned by Marcion's position, Hermogenes might be recognized as one of the greatest early Christian theologians. But as it was, his warning—that the idea of *creatio ex nihilo* would make it impossible to explain the origin of evil, at least without implying that God's goodness is less than perfect—has been borne out by the history of theodicy, as I have argued at great length.[43]

3 Traditional Theism's Problem of Evil

The traditional "problem of evil" can be formulated thus:

1. God is, by definition, omnipotent and perfectly good.

2. Being omnipotent, God *could* unilaterally prevent all evil.

3. Being perfectly good, God would *want* to prevent all evil.

4. However, evil does occur.

5. Therefore, God (thus defined) does not exist.

Because this argument is sound, the conclusion can be avoided only by denying one of these premises.

Evil could be explained, as Hermogenes suggested, by denying the second premise: Although he would probably have said that God is "omnipotent" in the sense of having all the power a creator could possibly have, Hermogenes held that creatures have inherent power to resist the divine will, which they have by virtue of the primordial stuff from which they were made.

The doctrine of *creatio ex nihilo*, however, closes off that option by implying (1) that the creatures have no inherent power with which to offer any resistance to the divine will, and (2) that there are no metaphysical principles, inherent in the nature of things, that reflect the kinds of relations that necessarily obtain either between God and the creatures or among the creatures themselves.

These two implications lie behind the traditional doctrine of omnipotence, according to which God can unilaterally bring about any possible state of affairs, providing that such states of affairs do not contain anything self-contradictory, such as round squares, or anything that could not without self-contradiction be unilaterally brought about by God, such as the free decisions of creatures.

The most important implication of this view is that God could unilaterally bring about a world that is just like ours except for having an absence of at least most of the things that we normally consider unnecessary evils, such as cancer, rape, murder, genocide, earthquakes, nuclear weapons, hurricanes, tornadoes, and climate change. Traditional theism's problem of evil is why our world has seemingly unnecessary evils. Its answers to the problem come in two versions of traditional theism: the all-determining and the free-will versions.

TRADITIONAL ALL-DETERMINING THEISM

According to this first version, as its name indicates, literally every event and feature of the world — whether in the physical world or the human mind — is fully determined by God. Although advocates of this position affirm that human beings are free in the sense of being responsible for their actions, their freedom is said somehow to be compatible with the fact that all of their actions, thoughts, and feelings are fully determined by God.

One approach has been to reject the third premise, that "God would *want* to avoid all evil." The argument begins with the observation that many things that are generally considered evil actually lead to great goods that would have been impossible without them: Pain created by the dentist is necessary for healthy teeth later on; poverty provides the opportunity for charity; sins against others provide them the opportunity for forgiveness; suffering can promote compassion; and so on. Accordingly, many things that may seem evil at first glance, which can be called *prima facie* evils, are not *genuinely* evil, defined as occurrences that make the universe worse than it might otherwise have been, all things considered. The argument's conclusion is that this realization, that some *prima facie* evils are only apparently evil, applies to all *prima facie* evils whatsoever, so that there is no genuine evil.

This conclusion means that the all-determining theist is thereby denying not the third premise, but the fourth — that "evil does occur." Confusion about which premise is being denied can be avoided by inserting the word "genuine" before "evil" in premises 2, 3, and 4. This insertion turns the third premise into a truism, because a perfectly good being would *by definition* want to prevent all genuine evil, meaning anything that would make the world worse than it might have been. All-determining theists can logically avoid the conclusion that God does not exist, therefore, only by denying the fourth premise, that "genuine evil exists" — which is what Leibniz did in declaring ours to be "the best of all possible worlds."[44]

However, as I have argued elsewhere, this denial is not one that we can make consistently — that is, without contradicting what we presuppose in practice — because in our daily living we all presuppose that less than optimal events occur. People can, of course, *verbally* deny that things happen without which the world would have been better. They can *say* that everything happens for the best. But not *in practice* — not in their attitudes, emotions, and actions.

When parents learn that their son has died in the hospital because of a careless physician's erroneous diagnosis, or a man learns that his wife and daughters have been raped and murdered, the emotional reactions of even the staunchest Calvinists will show that they do not really believe — in the sense of believing it in practice — that everything happens for the best. Voltaire's *Candide* was devoted, of course, to showing that a young man could not get through life believing that "everything happens for the best in this best of all possible worlds."[45]

An analogy is provided by the fact that we all presuppose in practice that we have a degree of freedom, in the sense that, after we choose A, it remains true that we *could have chosen* B or C. Of course, many people have denied that that genuine freedom exists, claiming that our *feeling* of freedom is an illusion. But making this verbal claim is not the same as living in practice as if everything we and other people do is completely determined, whether by our creator above or our molecules below. For example, philosopher John Searle has argued that free will is impossible:

> Since nature consists of particles and their relations with each other, and since everything can be accounted for in terms of those particles and their relations, there is simply no room for freedom of the will.

However, he said, "we can't act otherwise than on the assumption of freedom, no matter how much we learn about how the world works as a determined physical system," because "the conviction of freedom . . . is built into every normal, conscious, intentional action."[46]

Accordingly, just as we cannot help presupposing freedom, we cannot help presupposing that genuine evil occurs, even if we deny it verbally. So all-determining theism, by implying that God has unnecessarily brought about genuine evil, in effect denies the perfect goodness of God, as Hermogenes warned.

TRADITIONAL FREE WILL THEISM

Some traditional theists, recognizing that all-determining theism cannot provide a satisfactory answer, have developed a free-will version. It holds that although God *essentially* has all the power, God has, through a self-limitation, *voluntarily* given freedom to at least some of the creatures (human beings and perhaps some other rational creatures, such as angels), freedom with which they can act contrary to the will of God. This idea of a voluntary self-limitation on divine omnipotence is necessary because free-will theists (rightly) reject the "compatibilism" of all-determining theism, according to which creaturely freedom is somehow compatible with divine determinism.

The basic idea is that, although this freedom allows genuine evils—namely, sin and the evils resulting therefrom—to occur, the fact *that* such evils occur is itself not genuinely evil, because a world with genuinely free creatures, who can freely choose the right and the good, is a better world than a world that, while not afflicted by most of the things that we normally consider evil, would be devoid of the values that are made possible by genuine freedom. It is a better world because freely developed moral and religious virtues are important enough to outweigh all the problems resulting from the freedom that allows them. But this answer suffers from many problems, two of which will be mentioned here.

First, because traditional free will theists usually regard human beings as the only earthly creatures with freedom, it provides no answer to the question of what are usually called "natural evils," understood as those that are experienced by living creatures not capable of developing moral and religious values.

Second, according to traditional free-will theism, God could intervene to prevent any specific instance of evil: God could have diverted every bullet headed toward a person "too young to die" and could have prevented any of the massacres that have occurred; God could, in fact, prevent any sinful human intention from producing its intended effects. And God could prevent any disease or any natural disaster from producing permanent injury or premature death.

Even if we grant that our world, with its genuine freedom and correlative genuine evils, was the best choice, this freedom could always be temporarily interrupted. Defenders of this position rightly point out that, given our normal understanding of human beings as genuinely free, God's interruption of someone's freedom would mean that that person in that moment would not be fully human. To have violated Hitler's freedom would have violated his full humanity. In response, however, the critic can ask: Would not this violation have been a small price to pay to have prevented Hitler from violating the freedom and humanity of millions of other people?

Traditional free will theism, therefore, retains the assumption of all-determining theism that has led millions to question the existence, or at least the goodness, of a divine being. If there were a

Superman who could prevent all these kinds of events but refused to do so—perhaps on the grounds that doing so would "prevent opportunities for human growth"—we would consider him a monster. A Superman, of course, could not prevent most genuine evils, because, being finite, he could not be everywhere at once. But the God of traditional theism, being ubiquitous, does not have this excuse.

Faced with these problems, some classical free will theists simply say that, although they cannot explain why God allows so much evil, they need not do so. "If God is good and powerful as the theist believes," says Alvin Plantinga, "then he will indeed have a good reason for permitting evil; but why suppose the theist must be in a position to figure out what it is?"

Plantinga's answer here is part of his claim that theists need not offer a *theodicy,* which would attempt to provide a *plausible* explanation for the world's evils, but need provide only a *defense,* which merely shows that there is *no logical contradiction* between holding that "evil exists" and that "God is omnipotent, omniscient, and wholly good." However, a contentment with such a minimalist view of theological rationality seems to be based on the assumption that traditional theism is somehow in a privileged position, which it no longer is. Any theological view nowadays can commend itself only in terms of plausibility as well as self-consistency.[47]

In sum, traditional theism has an insoluble problem of evil because of its acceptance of the postbiblical doctrine of *creatio ex nihilo.*

4 A Process Theodicy

The problem of evil can be avoided only by some version of nontraditional theism, such as the process theism integral to Alfred North Whitehead's process philosophy.[48] Like traditional theism, process theism affirms the existence of a personal creator who is perfect in both power and goodness, but it is nontraditional by virtue of affirming a contemporary version of the biblical and Platonic notion of creation out of chaos and thereby a different understanding of divine power.

FROM "STUFF" TO CREATIVITY WITH SPONTANEITY

In the ancient visions of creation out of chaos, the "stuff" out of which our world was created was generally thought of as passive matter. As such, it could not actively offer resistance to a divine will. Nevertheless, a divine artisan would not necessarily be able to turn it into whatever might be desired, nor be able to go beyond what the matter made possible—just as, we say, one cannot "make a silk purse out of a sow's ear." (This seems to be the thought behind Plato's notion that the divine demiurge made the world as "good as possible.")

In process theism, by contrast, the stuff out of which our world was created is not what we normally think of as "stuff" at all, but creative activity. This idea is based in part on recent physics, according to which what we think of as "matter" consists of energy. Generalizing this notion, Whitehead referred to the stuff embodied in all individuals as "creativity." On this basis, the long-standing dualism between "physical nature" and "human experience" is overcome: All genuine individuals, from electrons to living cells to human beings, are understood as embodiments of creativity, or creative activity, which involves a degree of spontaneity.

It must be emphasized that spontaneity is attributed only to genuine individuals, not to "all things" whatsoever. The rock or piece of sand has no capacity for self-determination. Spontaneity belongs only to the genuine individuals making them up, such as their electrons, protons, atoms. The self-determinination and hence spontaneity of the individuals gets canceled out in aggregates such as rocks and sand by the law of large numbers. But this spontaneity of the tiny individuals is not cancelled out in living individuals, from single-celled organisms to the largest multicellular animals, because, over and above the tiny individuals, there is a higher-level individual, which can coordinate the spontaneities of all the constituent members of the animal body. This higher-level individual, which has a much greater degree of spontaneity, is the animal's psyche.

In human beings, the psyche's spontaneity becomes freedom. Just as we cannot help presupposing that we have a degree of freedom, we also commonly attribute a degree of spontaneity to other animals. Whitehead argued that we can intelligibly attribute at least an iota of such spontaneity all the way down. Some biologists now say that living cells have a degree of experience and spontaneity, and some quantum physicists say that absolute determinism cannot even be attributed to subatomic particles.[49]

DEGREES OF SPONTANEITY

Accordingly, rather than an absolute dualism between "humanity," with its freedom, and "nature," assumed to be rigidly determined, process philosophy suggests an evolutionary series of more or less radical differences of degree. In successively bringing forth atoms, molecules, prokaryotic cells, eukaryotic cells, multicelled animals, mammals, and human beings, the evolutionary process has brought forth beings with increasingly greater freedom.

The evolutionary development of our world can be understood to have begun, as suggested by Genesis, with a "formless void" or "chaos," because this development, by hypothesis, arose out of a primordial situation in which the creative activity was completely random, rather than being organized into enduring things, such as quarks, electrons, and protons.

People whose minds have been shaped by *creatio ex nihilo* will be inclined to ask where this chaos came from, contending that it must have been created by God. But what is the self-evident truth behind this *must*? It cannot be simply that "everything that exists must have been created," or else we would have to ask who created God. We do not ask this, because part of what we mean by "God" is "a being who exists necessarily." The correct formulation of the self-evident truth, therefore, is that "everything that exists contingently, rather than necessarily, must have been created." Given the obvious truth of *ex nihilo nihil fit*, traditional theists are quite right to hold that *something* must exist necessarily. The question is: What is this something?

Rather than being God alone, what exists necessarily, Whitehead suggested, is God-with-a-realm-of-finite-existents, perhaps in a chaotic state. In fact, as May points out, Hermogenes used the biblical designation of God as "Lord" to support this view, arguing that "God was in his unchangeableness always Lord, and so there must have been from eternity something for him to be Lord of."[50]

In a similar way, Whitehead said that, just as finite existents presuppose God, God also presupposes a realm of finite existents. Likewise, according to Whitehead our world arose out of Middle Platonism's "three principles": (1) God, (2) Ideas (called by Whitehead "eternal objects"), such as mathematical numbers, and (3) matter reconceived as "creativity." However this transformation of matter into creativity implied that there must be *four* eternal principles, because creativity eternally exists both as *divine*, embodied in God, and *creaturely* creativity, embodied in finite existents.

Accordingly, although God did not create our world "out of nothing" in traditional theism's sense, God did create things out of a situation of no-thing, in which there were finite existents but no enduring things, not even quarks.

DIVINE POWER AS PERSUASIVE, NOT CONTROLLING

One implication of this view is that power is always *shared* power. If God is the supreme but never the only embodiment of creativity, then God has never had a monopoly on power. Also, because the creativity embodied in finite beings is inherent to the realm of finitude, this creativity cannot be withdrawn or overridden. Human freedom is, to be sure, a gift from God, brought about through billions of years of evolutionary development. But because it was evoked out of the capacity for spontaneity inherent in worldly existents as well as God, human freedom, now that it exists, cannot be simply withdrawn.

This view of shared power implies, in turn, that divine power is persuasive, not controlling. Although God, by hypothesis, influences every creature, God cannot wholly determine how creatures will use their own power. Accordingly, as Plato and Hermogenes suggested, our creator could only bring about the best order possible.

NECESSARY CORRELATIONS BETWEEN VALUE AND POWER

Given Middle Platonism's and Whitehead's "eternal principles," it makes sense to suppose that there are some necessary principles, inherent in the very nature of things, about the nature of finite existents, their relations to each other, and their relations to God. Two of these principles have already been implied: that all existents, by virtue of embodying creativity, have spontaneity and also the power to influence other existents; and that even the supreme existent can never override the exercise by other existents of their power.

A third principle is that correlations necessarily obtain among the following variables: (1) The capacity to enjoy positive value. (2) The capacity to suffer negative value (evil). (3) The power of self-determination. (4) The power to influence others, for good or ill. To say that a positive correlation exists means that, as one variable increases, all the others increase proportionately.

Because of these necessary correlations, it would not have been possible for God to have created beings similar to ourselves, having the same capacity to enjoy positive value, but with less capacity to suffer evil, or less power to inflict it on others. Accordingly, Whitehead has helped us to see how the creator of our world could be perfectly good. We cannot reasonably expect God to have done the impossible.

6 Conclusion

Process theodicy shows how, in particular, climate change could destroy human civilization, even though our world was produced by a creator with perfect power and goodness. The possibility of such destruction would not prove the truth of atheism, because reasonable theism does not mean that human civilization is divinely protected.

By contrast, traditional theism, with its *creatio ex nihilo*, has convinced many people, including many U.S. politicians, that we need not worry about continuing to burn fossil fuels, because civilization will not be destroyed unless God wants this.

Besides being verified by the history of theodicy, Hermogenes' warning of the dangers of *creatio ex nihilo* has recently received its highest demonstration, because traditional theism now threatens to contribute to the ultimate genocide — the suicide of the human race.

Notes

1   Elizabeth May, "Can Civilization Survive Climate Change?" Killam Lecture, Dalhousie University, Halifax, Nova Scotia, 24 August 2006.

2   Elizabeth Kolbert, *Field Notes from a Catastrophe: Man, Nature, and Climate Change* (Bloomsbury, 2006), 189.

3   Lester R. Brown, "The Geopolitics of Food Scarcity," *Der Spiegel Online*, 11 February 2009.

4   The Blue Planet Laureates, "Environment and Development Challenges: The Imperative to Act," 20 February 2012.

5   Noam Chomsky and Andre Vitchek, *On Western Terrorism: From Hiroshima to Drone Warfare* (Pluto Press, 2013), 2.

6   Richard L. Rubenstein, *After Auschwitz: Radical Theology and Contemporary Judaism* (Bobbs-Merrill, 1966); William R. Jones, *Is God a White Racist? A Preamble to Black Theology* (Anchor Press, 1973).

7   Millard J. Erickson, *Christian Theology* (Baker Book House, 1985), 304.

8   Ibid., 54.

9   "Climate Change: Key Data Points from Pew Research," Pew Research Center, 2 April 2013; Max Fisher, "Americans Are Less Worried about Climate Change than Almost Anyone Else," *Washington Post*, 27 September 2013.

10 Frank Newport, "In U.S., 46% Hold Creationist View of Human Origins," Gallup, 1 June 2012.

11 "Evangelicals Support Some Climate Change Policies," *Conservation Magazine*, June 2013, referring to Neil Smith and Anthony Leiserowitz, "American Evangelicals and Global Warming," *Global Environmental Change*, 28 May 2013.

12 Senator James Inhofe, *The Greatest Hoax: How the Global Warming Conspiracy Threatens Your Future* (WND Books, 2012), 70–71.

13 Brian Tashman, "James Inhofe Says the Bible Refutes Climate Change," Right Wing Watch, 3 August 2012.

14 "God Won't Allow Global Warming, Congressman Seeking to Head Energy Committee Says," Raw Story, 11 November 2010.

15 David Edwards, "Limbaugh: Christians 'Cannot Believe in Man-made Global Warming,'" Raw Story, 14 August 2013.

16 David C. Barker and David H. Bearce, "End-Times Theology, the Shadow of the Future, and Public Resistance to Addressing Global Climate Change," *Political Research Quarterly*, June 2013.

17 K. C. Boyd, "The End-Times Politics of Pastor John Hagee," AlterNet, 29 January 2013.

18 Ryan Chiachiere and Kathleen Henehan, "Will MSNBC Devote as Much Coverage to McCain's Embrace of Hagee's Support as It Did to Obama's Rejection of Farrakhan?" *Media Matters*, 28 February 2008.

19 David Crowe, "Katrina: God's Judgment on America," Beliefnet, September 2005.

20 Molly Redden, "Whatever Happened to the Evangelical-Environmental Alliance?" *New Republic*, 3 November 2011.

21 John Calvin, *Institutes of the Christian Religion*, ed. John T. McNeill, trans. Ford Lewis Battles (Westminster Press, 1960), III, xxiii, 7.

22 Martin Luther, *On the Bondage of the Will*, trans. J. I. Packer and O. R. Johnston (Fleming H. Revell Company, 1957), 80.

23 St. Augustine, *Enchiridion*, trans. J. F. Shaw, XLI, XLII; in *Basic Writings of St. Augustine,* 2 vols., ed. Whitney J. Oates (Random House, 1948).

24 Erickson, *Christian Theology,* 374.

25 Jon D. Levenson, *Creation and the Persistence of Evil: The Jewish Drama of Divine Omnipotence* (Harper & Row, 1988), 121.

26 Ibid., 121, 157, n. 12.

27 Ibid., 12, 26, 122–23.

28 Gerhard May, *Creatio Ex Nihilo: The Doctrine of "Creation out of Nothing" in Early Christian Thought,* translated by A. S. Worrall (T. & T. Clark, 1994), xi, 27.

29 Ibid., viii, xii, 25–26, 77, 150, 161, 174.

30 Ibid., 3–4.

31 Ibid., 77.

32 Ibid., 6, 12, 25.

33 Ibid., xiii, 25, 61, 74, 122.

34 Ibid., xiii, 4, 24.

35 Ibid., 40, 43, 56.

36 Ibid., 43, 56n, 61, 152. It is important to realize, in addition, that when the doctrine of *creatio ex nihilo* was affirmed by the Fourth Lateran Council in 1215, it was directed against Catharism, which held Manichean doctrines of matter and creation similar to those of Marcion; see Jeffrey Burton Russell, *Lucifer: The Devil in the Middle Ages* (Cornell University Press, 1984), 189.

37 Ibid., 140, 141, 142, 145, 146.

38 Ibid., 144, 142.

39 Ibid., 140, 146.

40 Ibid., 147, 161.

41 Ibid., 147, 167-68, 174, 177.

42 Ibid., 178.

43 *God, Power, and Evil: A Process Theodicy* (Westminster, 1976); reprinted with a new preface 1991 (University Press of America); reprinted with a newer preface 2004 (Westminster John Knox); *Evil Revisited: Responses and Reconsiderations* (State University of New York Press, 1991); "Creation out of Chaos and the Problem of

Evil," in Stephen T. Davis, ed., *Encountering Evil: Live Options in Theodicy* (John Knox, 1981), plus responses to other contributors; "Process Theology and the Christian Good News: A Response to Classical Free Will Theism," and "In Response to William Hasker," in John B. Cobb Jr. and Clark H. Pinnock, eds., *Searching for an Adequate God: A Dialogue between Process and Free Will Theists* (Eerdmans, 2000), 1–38 and 246–62; "Traditional Free Will Theodicy and Process Theodicy: Hasker's Claim for Parity," *Process Studies* 29/2 (Fall-Winter 2000), 209–26; "On Hasker's Attempt to Defend His Parity Claim," *Process Studies* 29/2 (Fall-Winter 2000), 233–36.

44 Griffin, *God, Power, and Evil*, Ch. 11.

45 This argument is made at length in my *Reenchantment Without Supernaturalism: A Process Philosophy of Religion* (Cornell University Press, 2000), Ch. 6.

46 John R. Searle, *Minds, Brains, and Science: The 1984 Reith Lectures* (British Broadcasting Corporation, 1984), 86, 97. I have made this argument more fully in Griffin, *Religion and Scientific Naturalism: Overcoming the Conflicts* (State University of New York Press, 2000), Ch. 6.

47 Alvin Plantinga, "Reply to the Basingers on Divine Omnipotence," *Process Studies* 11/1 (Spring, 1981): 25–29, at 26–28.

48 A summary of the core doctrines of process philosophy is provided in the introduction to my *Reenchantment Without Supernaturalism*.

49 See John B. Cobb Jr. and David Ray Griffin, "Lynn Margulis on Spirituality and Process Philosophy," in Dorion Sagan, ed., *Lynn Margulis: The Life and Legacy of a Scientific Rebel* (Chelsea Green, 2012); and "Introduction: The Reenchantment of Science," in David Ray Griffin, ed., *The Reenchantment of Science: Postmodern Proposals* (State University of New York Press, 1988).

50 May, *Creatio Ex Nihilo*, 141.

CHAPTER SEVEN

Divine Goodness and Demonic Evil

R ELIGION HAS TO DO PRIMARILY with the desire to overcome evil through proper relation to the supreme power of the universe. This characterization of religion reflects my own perspective, which is theistic, but I believe that it applies more broadly. To the extent that it does, religion in general presupposes belief in both worldly evil and divine goodness. The problem of evil in most general terms is how to reconcile what we believe about the goodness and power of the divine reality of the universe with the evil of our world. The previous chapter shows how Whitehead's ideas can be used to overcome that problem of evil. The present chapter discusses the form of evil that I call "demonic."

1 Demonic Evil

With this term, I point to evil that diametrically opposes divine power and does so with such strength as to destroy divine creations in a way that threatens divine purposes.

Because this definition puts the demonic in direct opposition to divine power, fleshing out this purely formal definition requires a positive characterization of the divine power.

My threefold characterization of divine power is power that is (1) always employed persuasively and creatively, (2) always based on responsive love for the creatures, and therefore (3) always informed by creative love, which means that it always intends the good of those upon whom it is exerted.

Given this idea of divine power, we can characterize the demonic as power that is (1) employed coercively and destructively (as well as perhaps persuasively and creatively), (2) based on hate and/or indifference towards at least some of those upon whom it is exercised, and, therefore, (3) not aimed at the good of all those upon whom it is exercised. This threefold characterization explains how demonic evil is diametrically opposed to divine power. The other condition for its being truly demonic is that it be strong enough to destroy divine creations in a way that threatens divine purposes.

The New Testament contained a realistic but mythical view of demonic evil. It must be considered mythical, in the pejorative sense, because the demonic was portrayed in terms of an actual individual—Satan, the devil—who rivals God in cosmic scope, knowledge, and power, thereby having powers that no creature could have. This picture was realistic, however, in that it did justice to the extent to which the world seems to be under the sway of a demonic force. Rather than sanguinely regarding divine goodness as in control of all events, the New Testament speaks of the devil as "the ruler of this world" (John 14:30, 16:11 RSV) and "the god of this age" (II Cor. 4:4 RSV). It also says that "the whole world is in the power of the evil one" (I Jn. 5:19 RSV) and has the devil say that the kingdoms of the world are under his control (Lk. 4:5–6 RSV). The battle between the divine and the demonic powers is regarded as a real battle, upon which the fate of the world depends.

To be sure, the New Testament also stated that "the present evil age" (Gal. 1:4 RSV) was coming to an end, thanks to the inbreaking of the rule of God in the life, death, and resurrection of Jesus. But, in whatever sense we may regard the divine reality's activity in Jesus as the beginning of the end of demonic control of our planet, it is empirically obvious that this was at most only a beginning.

2 The Growth of Demonic Evil

Indeed, demonic control of the planet has increased qualitatively during the intervening 2000 years, especially in the past four centuries, which we call the modern age. War in the 20th and 21st centuries has involved unprecedented slaughter of human beings. And this slaughter could have been even greater, thanks to the most obvious manifestation of demonic power in these centuries, the building and upgrading of thousands of nuclear weapons, through which all human life and much of the rest of the planet's life could have been destroyed in hours—a threat that has by no means been removed.

Furthermore, even if we do avoid nuclear holocaust, the present trajectory of civilization, with its increasing population, consumerism, and ever-increasing use of fossil fuels, promises unprecedented suffering through scarcity and climate change sometime in the 21st century.[1]

The projections based upon purely ecological matters are bad enough; when this growing scarcity of land, food, and other resources is combined with increasing ethnic and cultural animosities, the proliferation of nuclear weapons, and arms sales generally, any realistic picture of the future based on present trends is completely terrifying. We live in a world that is essentially good, created by divine power. But it is a world that is, even more fully than was the world in New Testament times, presently in the grip of demonic power.

3 A Non-Mythical but Realistic View of Demonic Evil

To have a theology that is adequate to reality, we need a way of formulating the New Testament's realistic portrayal of the demonic while discarding its mythology. We have not inherited such an account, however, because traditional theology did just the opposite: It retained the mythical aspect of the New Testament's portrayal of the demonic while giving up its realism.

MONISTIC MONOTHEISM

In St. Augustine's theology, for example, Satan is an individual center of consciousness and will. Given Augustine's view of divine omnipotence as actually causing everything that occurs, however, he could not allow for any creaturely center of power that could truly act counter to the divine will. He said: "Nothing . . . happens unless the Omnipotent wills it to happen." Augustine does not flinch from applying this doctrine to sinful thoughts and actions, saying that God "does in the hearts of even wicked men whatsoever He wills." Augustine explicitly applied this doctrine to the devil. In speaking of the afflictions of Job and the temptations of Peter, he said: "God himself . . . did all things justly by the power he gave to the devil."[2]

The battle between the divine and the demonic is, accordingly, a mock, not a real, battle. The demonic is entirely under the divine thumb. The realism of the New Testament image of the demonic is lost in the theology of Augustine and other classical theologians because of their monistic monotheism, according to which there is only one center of power.

SEMIDUALISTIC MONOTHEISM

The New Testament's view, by contrast, was what historian Jeffrey Russell, in his books on the relation of God to a demonic power, has called "semidualistic monotheism."[3] Semidualism is not a full-fledged dualism, which would be contrary to biblical monotheism. The demonic power is neither another cosmic individual alongside God nor is it co-eternal with God: It is a creature, a rather late-arriving one at that, having not existed for most of the history of our universe or even most of the 4.6 billion-year history of our planet. However, now that it has been created (like everything else, through divine-creaturely cooperation), it is, unlike Augustine's Satan, not completely controllable by God. This is because demonic power, while not itself eternal, is (by hypothesis) rooted in an eternal power: creativity.

To clarify: Monistic monotheism involves the hypothesis that creative power is eternally instantiated only in a Divine Individual. Atheism usually involves the opposite hypothesis: that creative power is eternally instantiated only in a plurality of nondivine entities or processes. Semidualistic monotheism, by contrast, holds that creative power eternally has both Divine and nondivine instantiations.

This aspect of the doctrine also does not entail a full-fledged, anti-monotheistic dualism: Creaturely power as such is not another individual, alongside God. It also is not inherently evil, but neutral, being capable of being used either to build or to destroy.

This doctrine also does not entail that *our* world is eternal; it arose, according to recent calculations, some 14 billion years ago. It only entails that there have always been *some* finite embodiments of creativity (or energy), so that our world arose not out of absolute nothingness, but out of a prior state—perhaps chaotic—of energetic events.

According to this hypothesis, although God did not create creaturely creativity "once upon a time," God did, in a strong sense, bring into existence our particular universe.[4] God is also *our* creator in a strong sense: Without the whole history of divine influence through which life, animal life, mammals, and then primates emerged, the existence of human beings would not have been possible. The emergence of human beings as such, furthermore, involved (by hypothesis) fresh divine influence. So, although the bare existence of creaturely power is not contingent upon a divine volition (being instead necessitated by the Divine Existence), our distinctively human set of powers *is* a gift of God.

This means that demonic power is a creature of God: Although God did not directly create it, God created its preconditions by creating human beings. This doctrine does not imply that God is indictable: Given the metaphysical principles, humanlike beings could not be created without the possibility that their power would become demonic. It does imply, however, that when this eventuality came about, God could not simply undo it: Although demonic power is a contingent emergence, it is an extreme instantiation of a power that is not contingent.

The creation of human beings was, accordingly, an extremely risky venture. Although they would be able to realize far greater values than could any of the previous creatures on our plane, those previous creatures were capable of realizing real, nontrivial values. The ecological balance of the planet, furthermore, is such that these other millions of species could continue realizing these values for a very long time.

The creation of human beings, however, meant the introduction into the ecosphere of creatures having the wherewithal to develop the power, within a hundred thousand years or so (depending upon where one dates the "first humans"), to destroy most of these other forms of life. The crucial period for determining how this experiment turns out will likely be the 21st century—which gives those of us alive now our unique privilege and awesome responsibility.

That, however, is to get ahead of the story. Having seen how demonic power is ontologically possible in a monotheistic universe, the next question is how this possibility became historically actualized.

4 The Possibility of Demonic Power

Demonic power became possible on this planet with the rise of human beings. Because of the human being's dual power to grasp things, both physically and conceptually, the rise of human beings meant the rise of a kind of creaturely power that could for the first time diametrically and strongly oppose the power of our creator. Because of our unprecedented power of self-determination, we can make decisions that run strongly counter to the divine influences upon us, which are always calling us to truth, beauty, and goodness. With humans, the power to know the difference between good and evil, and thereby the power of sin, entered the world.

Because of our ability to manipulate symbols with our minds and physical objects with our hands, we also have far more power to exert coercive power than do other creatures. Our power to sin is matched by an equally unprecedented power to dominate. Our unprecedented power of influence is not limited, however, to coercion: Our linguistic ability has given us an unprecedented form of persuasive power as well, a form of power that was greatly augmented with the invention of writing. These unique abilities of human beings are necessary conditions for the rise of demonic power.

Above, I characterized demonic power not merely in terms of its nature and strength, but also in terms of its being employed on the basis of hate or indifference and thereby in a destructive way. This aspect of the possibility for the emergence of demonic power is rooted in our nature as creatures. Because we, unlike God, are local rather than all-inclusive beings, our sympathies tend to be very restricted. We can be indifferent about the welfare of most other creatures and positively antagonistic to the welfare of those whom we perceive to be threats to our own welfare. We do, to be sure, have the capacity to objectify ourselves, to realize thereby that we are simply one among many creatures, all of whom are creatures of the same creator, all of whom have feelings and interests. And we have the capacity to be aware of moral norms, such as the principle that equals should be treated equally, that we should do to others as we would have them do to us.

But we likewise have the capacity to use our same intellectual capacities to ignore these norms when convenient, or so to qualify and circumscribe them that they become virtually inapplicable to all except those with whom we naturally sympathize. Rather than using these capacities to overcome our natural indifference or antagonism to others, in fact, we can use them to create a hostility towards others that greatly surpasses in intensity, extent, and duration anything found in the nonhuman world. It is our very humanity, in short, that creates the possibility for the emergence of demonic power.

In rejecting the mythical idea of the demonic as a devil, I have indicated that the demonic is not an individual being. There is no evil soul alongside the divine soul of the universe. But the demonic is not, on the other hand, simply the aggregated power of individual human beings. It consists, instead, of what can be called a quasi-soul.

The Whiteheadian idea of creativity, on which I am building, provides a way to explicate what Walter Rauschenbusch, in giving a non-mythical account of original sin in his *Theology for the Social Gospel*, called the supra-personal power of evil.[5] Rauschenbusch described the structures and habits that promote sin, describing how people are seduced into sin, through the power of authority and imitation, long before they have reached the age of accountability. To all that Rauschenbusch says, we can add a form of influence that works at a presensory level and at a distance.

The science of psychical research, or parapsychology, has amply demonstrated that such influence occurs.[6] Evidence for telepathy and clairvoyance show that we have the capacity to receive causal influence at a distance. Evidence for psychokinesis shows that we have the capacity to exert this kind of causal influence. Modern science, philosophy, and theology have, however, largely ignored this evidence, because it did not fit with the reigning worldview.

The early modern worldview, with its mechanistic view of nature and its sensationist view of perception, said that such influence cannot occur except through supernatural intervention. The late modern worldview, by retaining early modernity's view of nature and perception while rejecting its supernaturalism, has said that such influence cannot happen at all. This late modern worldview has made extrasensory perception and psychokinetic influence seem all the more impossible by regarding the mind as epiphenomenal, that is, as a mere byproduct of the brain without any autonomous power of its own to exert power or to perceive. Modern theology, accepting the modern worldview's veto, has ignored parapsychology's offer of empirical evidence supporting the reality of spiritual influence.

By contrast, Whitehead's worldview, while rejecting supernaturalism, allows for the reality of this spiritual influence at a distance. Because the world is made of events of creative experience, rather than bits of insentient matter, there is no reason to suppose that causal influence can be exerted only by contact and therefore only on contiguous things. Also, the idea that all individuals enjoy a nonsensory form of perception, so that sensory perception is derivative from this more primordial, nonsensory mode of perception, means that extrasensory perception, whether telepathic or clairvoyant, does not need to be regarded as a violation of the laws of nature. Reports of such occurrences need not, accordingly, be regarded as either fraudulent or as evidence of supernatural intervention.

Rather, events in which people become aware of extrasensory perception can be regarded as simply the consciousness of a kind of nonsensory perception that is occurring all the time. What is exceptional about such perceptions is not that they involve nonsensory perception, but only that a form of perception that usually remains unconscious has risen to the conscious level of experience.

Furthermore, this worldview, far from regarding the human mind or soul as impotent, regards it as the most powerful creature on the face of the earth. The parapsychological evidence that the human mind can directly exert far more influence on other things beyond its body, including other minds, than can other animals is, accordingly, what should be expected. Cases of reported psychokinesis can be regarded as merely conspicuous instances of a kind of pervasive psychic influence that is radiating from our minds all the time.

From this perspective, we can suppose that we are influencing each other directly, soul to soul, all the time. And we can suppose that through the enormously complex web of psychic influence that results, we are born into a kind of quasi-soul, which shapes our souls for good or for ill, and to which we in turn contribute, thereby adding our influence, for good or for ill, to the psychic ether that will shape other souls.

This influence at a distance is, of course, usually quite weak in comparison with physically mediated influence. There is a factor, however, that somewhat balances out the power of these two kinds of influence on us. The "distance" over which this kind of influence operates can be temporal as well as spatial distance. Because of this influence over time, repetitions of a certain form of activity can have a cumulative effect.

For example, if a certain image has been focused upon by devotees of a particular religion for hundreds, perhaps thousands, of years, this image will be impressed upon the unconscious portion of the psyches of present-day individuals with considerable power. This, incidentally, is a way of explaining the reality and power of Jungian archetypes, a way that Jung himself sometimes employed.[7] Rupert Sheldrake's "new science of life" is also based on the cumulative effects of repetition.[8]

Through this idea, we can see how the demonic could be an even stronger power than Rauschenbusch thought. Everything he said about the power of the written word, pictures, patriotic songs, history books, examples, stereotypes, ideologies, and so on, would stand. To all this we can add the reinforcing power that comes from the hate and other violence-inducing attitudes, emotions, and images that have been repeated countless times down through human history. What Rauschenbusch called a "kingdom of evil," into which we are born, can be imagined as a demonic quasi-soul, that not only influences us indirectly, through our sensory experience, but also directly, through spiritual influence.

This completes my account of how demonic power could have arisen in a monotheistic universe, in the sense of how it is ontologically possible. The next topic is the historical process through which this demonic possibility came to dominance on this planet, so that it now threatens to destroy the finest products on our planet of billions of years of divine creative activity.

5 The Demonic's Historical Rise to Ascendancy

My ideas in this section have been inspired primarily by Andrew Bard Schmookler's book *The Parable of the Tribes*.[9] Schmookler's view of the central importance of the war-system in shaping the direction taken by civilization over the past 10,000 years has been reinforced by writings of William H. McNeill.[10] A position on the demonic similar to mine was also developed in Walter Wink's trilogy on the powers, especially the third volume, *Engaging the Powers*.[11]

The basic idea of this new perspective is that the war-system, along with the more general domination system, began within the past 10,000 years. It was occasioned by the rise of civilization, with its cities and agriculture—which had been allowed by the birth of the Holocene epoch, with its ideal climate for human civilization. During the prior 40,000 years of the existence of homo sapiens sapiens, life was surely filled with evils of various sorts. Desires of revenge and other motives surely would have led tribes to carry out savage raids on each other from time to time. But the hunting-and-gathering mode of existence would have provided no motive for a war-system as such. For example, captives, who could not be entrusted to share in the hunt, would simply provide more mouths to feed.

But the rise of civilization changed all this. Slaves could be assigned the drudge work involved in agriculture and the building of walls and water canals. Women captives could, besides working in the homes and the fields, bear children to build up the city's defensive and offensive capacity. The cities, their cultivated lands, and their domesticated herds also provided motives for attack. The rise of civilization brought the institutionalization of war.

Once the war-system began, everyone was forced to participate. Even if most societies wanted to be peaceful, any one society could force the rest to prepare for war or risk being subjugated or annihilated. As Schmookler said, "Nice guys are finished first."[12]

In this war-system, it is power, not morality, that determines the relations among the states. As stated in the Hobbesian analysis, the interstate realm is a state of anarchy: There is no superior power to declare and enforce any moral norms. Might rather literally makes right. The classic formulation is provided by Thucydides, who has the Athenian general limit the Meletans' choices to being taken over peacefully or violently, adding that if they had the superior power they would do the same to the Athenians.

In this Hobbesian situation of the war of all against all—which means not that you actually fight against everyone else, but that every other society is at least potentially your enemy—war is not brought on only by the desire of one society's leaders for additional power, riches, and glory, but also by the fear that another society is amassing enough military power to attack them. Thucydides again provides the classic statement, having Alcibiades say, with regard to taking Sicily: "If we cease to rule others, we are in danger of being ruled ourselves."

In this anarchical state of civilization, coercive power inevitably grows. Each advance by any one state must be matched by advances by the others within striking distance. A move that may be intended defensively will often look offensive to others, evoking further efforts by them to increase their power. And there is no stopping point. Although the development of nuclear weapons might have occurred either sooner or considerably later than it actually did, the fact that it did eventually occur was made virtually inevitable by the dynamics of the system.

Of course, not every nation has tried to acquire a massive military complete with nuclear weapons. Some countries are too small and poor; countries have avoided being taken over by having no resources that others want to steal. As illustrated recently, the countries that have been attacked had large oil and gas reserves. Countries can also avoid being swallowed by forming alliances with a powerful neighbor, as when Syria avoided being taken over by means of its alliance with Russia.

In any case, the development of coercive power does not involve only the development of new forms of weapons and defenses. The most obvious additional element is military strategy and tactics. But a society's ability to wage war is also to a great extent a function of its political and economic systems. Any development that gives a society a temporary military edge, such as the 14th-century rise of capitalism in the Italian city-states, will tend to spread to the neighboring societies.

The main point of this analysis is that the evolution of civilization in the state of anarchy is necessarily shaped in large part by a principle similar to that of "survival of the fittest" based on natural selection in Darwinian evolution. Schmookler calls this principle the "selection for power." This analysis is not reductionistic, as if the drive for power were at the root of all cultural developments. The point is, instead, that of those developments that do occur, those that increase a society's power vis-à-vis other societies will tend not only to survive but also to spread. In the long run, the direction of civilization is shaped most decisively by this selection for power.

As civilization evolves, the need for power increasingly shapes every aspect of a society. In recent decades, for example, something like half of our nation's science has been devoted to military-related research. Anarchical civilization, with its war-system, results in a reign of power.

Implicit in this analysis is the idea that the reign of power in the interstate arena leads to the reign of power within each state. This is not to say that the rise of patriarchal, hierarchical, domination societies was motivated entirely or even primarily by the demands of the war-system. That interstate system did, however, provide the context in which hierarchical societies were virtually inevitable. As Gerda Lerner pointed out, nonhierarchical societies for the most part did not survive,[13] and it is hard to argue with the claim that survival must take priority over all other considerations. The argument from "necessity" in relation to external dangers has always, probably from the outset of the war-system, provided the excuse for the worst kinds of internal inequalities. The war-system has also provided an ever-increasing basis for the human domination of nature.

The foregoing is my suggestion as to how demonic power, which the rise of human existence made possible, actually came to dominance on our planet. Over the past 10,000 years, human civilization has increasingly been oriented around the drive to increase human power, in the sense of the power to control, to destroy, and to intimidate. Human beings in this context have wanted more power over nature in order to increase their power over other human groups, in order to give them more power over nature, and on and on. Civilization has been largely shaped by the drive to produce coercive power that would be used with hate or at least indifference—and this is our concept of the demonic. Civilization has especially and increasingly been in its grip for the past 5,000 years.

I have thus far, however, left out what is arguably the most important factor in this story. The power of a society is determined not only by the size of its armies, its military technology, strategies, and tactics, and its political and economic systems. Undergirding all of these dimensions is the ideology of a society, its theology. (Any all-inclusive ideology is a theology insofar as it involves, at least implicitly, a notion of that which is holy or sacred.) And, just as the selection for power operates with regard to all these other dimensions, it also operates in relation to ideologies.[14]

We should expect, accordingly, that the history of anarchical civilization's theologies and philosophies will involve the gradual ascendancy of those ideologies that are most effective in producing a warrior-mentality and thereby a warrior-society. An effective ideology of power may, for example, make people unafraid to die in battle and may even lead them to desire such a death; it may lead them to believe that by being warriors they are obeying the will, and even imitating the behavior, of the deity of the universe; it may lead them to hate, or at least be indifferent to, the welfare of people in other societies; it may convince them that they are a chosen people, so that by subjugating others they are actually bringing about divine rule on earth; and so on. An effective ideology of power may also tend to promote political and economic systems that increase a society's military capacity; it may also tend to develop philosophies, sciences, and technologies through which nature can be effectively dominated. The growth of such ideologies of power has been an intricate part — in many ways the most important part — of the growth of demonic power over the past few thousand years.

By the demonic, I mean the whole complex of belief-systems, symbols, images, stories, habits, attitudes, emotions, sciences, technologies, institutions, webs of direct and indirect psychic influence, and everything else that is oriented around the production and deployment of destructive power, used with hate or indifference, to dominate and destroy fellow creatures of God. This demonic power is now, even more completely than in New Testament times, in effective control of the trajectory of civilization.

Although religions should seek to respond in various ways to evil, and should respond to evil in all its forms, their primary concern should be to serve as an agency of the divine reality to overcome demonic evil. The above analysis of demonic evil implies that the effort by religious leaders to overcome demonic evil would have two primary foci: eliminating those aspects of our own religious traditions' theology that give support to the demonic, and working for the transcendence of global anarchy.

Notes

1   See my *Unprecedented: Can Civilization Survive the CO_2 Crisis?* (Clarity Press, 2015).

2   These statements by Augustine are from the *Enchiridion* XIV: 96,

XXIV:95, and *Grace and Free Will* XLII, which can be found in *Basic Writings of St. Augustine*, ed. Whitney J. Oates (Random House, 1953).

3   Jeffrey Burton Russell, *The Devil: Perceptions of Evil from Antiquity to Primitive Christianity* (Cornell University Press, 1977), 228, 248); *Satan: The Early Christian Tradition* (Cornell University Press, 1981), 32.

4   See David Ray Griffin, *God Exists but Gawd Does Not: From Evil to New Atheism to Fine-Tuning* (Process Century Press, 2016), Chapter 14, "Teleological Order."

5   See Walter Rauschenbusch, *A Theology for the Social Gospel* (Macmillan, 1918), especially the chapters on "The Super-Personal Forces of Evil" and "The Kingdom of Evil."

6   For excellent surveys of parapsychological studies, see Benjamin Wolman, ed., *Handbook of Parapsychology* (Van Nostrand Reinhold, 1977); Hoyt L. Edge, Robert L. Morris, John Palmer, and Joseph H. Rush, *Foundations of Parapsychology* (Routledge and Kegan Paul, 1986); and the series, *Advances in Parapsychological Research*, ed. Stanley Krippner (Plenum Press), especially Vol. I, *Psychokinesis* (1977) and Vol. II, *Extrasensory Perception* (1978). For evaluations of the evidence by capable philosophers, see *Essays on Psychical Research* in the Harvard edition of the writings of William James, ed. by Robert McDermott; C. D. Broad, *Religion, Philosophy and Psychical Research* (Routledge and Kegan Paul, 1953; Humanities Press, 1969); and Stephen Braude, *ESP and Psychokinesis: A Philosophical Examination* (Temple University Press, 1979) and *The Limits of Influence: Psychokinesis and the Philosophy of Science* (Routledge and Kegan Paul, 1986). See also my *Parapsychology, Philosophy, and Spirituality: A Postmodern Exploration* (State University of New York Press, 1997), and Chapter 7, "Parapsychology, Science, and Religion" in my *Religion and Scientific Naturalism: Overcoming the Conflicts* (State University of New York Press, 2000).

7   See my introduction to David Ray Griffin, ed., *Archetypal Process: Self and Divine in Whitehead, Jung, and Hillman* (Northwestern University Press, 1989), esp. 39–44.

8   Rupert Sheldrake, *A New Science of Life* (Blond and Briggs, 1981); *Science Set Free: 10 Paths to New Discovery* (Deepak Chopra, 2013).

9   Andrew Bard Schmookler, *The Parable of the Tribes: The Problem of Power in Social Evolution* (Houghton Mifflin, 1986).

10 See especially William H. McNeill, *The Rise of the West: A History of the Human Community* and *The Pursuit of Power: Technology, Armed Force, and Society since A.D. 1000* (The University of Chicago Press, 1982).

11 Walter Wink, *Engaging the Powers: Discernment and Resistance in a World of Domination* (Fortress Press, 1992).

12 Schmookler, *The Parable of the Tribes,* 45.

13 Gerda Lerner, *The Creation of Patriarchy* (Oxford University Press, 1986), 35.

14 Schmookler suggested that the selection for power would have also operated with regard to religious ideologies (*The Parable of the Tribes,* 73, 80), but he did not develop this idea.

CHAPTER EIGHT

Charles Hartshorne as Christian Theologian

CHARLES HARTSHORNE, ALONG WITH ALFRED NORTH WHITEHEAD, has been the chief influence on the movement known as process theology. Although he has thereby had a strong impact on Christian theology, it might be asked whether Hartshorne himself belonged in a handbook of Christian theologians — which was the case with the original essay on which the present chapter is based. Besides calling himself a philosopher, Hartshorne did not even portray himself as a specifically Christian philosopher.

1 Christian Natural Theology

However, Hartshorne's thought was devoted primarily to that branch of philosophy traditionally known as "natural theology." Also, it would not be inaccurate to call his position a "Christian natural theology." Although Hartshorne's thought is to be judged entirely in terms of philosophical criteria, it was decisively shaped by Christian intuitions, as he himself recognized.

For example, he said that the firmest residue from his pious upbringing is "summed up in the phrase Deus est caritas [God is love], together with the two 'Great Commandments': total love for God and love for neighbor comparable to love for self." To that, he added: "If there are central intuitive convictions back of my acceptance or rejection of philosophical doctrines, these may be the ones."[1]

As is appropriate for a philosopher who emphasizes the degree to which our experience, in spite of its own creative self-determination, is shaped by a multitude of influences, Hartshorne's autobiographical reflections are largely devoted to the experiences and people that shaped his attitudes and beliefs. In these reflections, he always stressed his "pious upbringing." His father was an Episcopalian priest; his mother was the daughter of an Episcopalian priest. Both of his parents not only believed that God is love and that love for God and fellow creatures sums up Christian ethics; they also lived out these beliefs, making a religion of love attractive. "From childhood," Hartshorne says, "I learned to worship divine love."[2]

Regarding the central principle of his philosophy—that "the love that 'moves the sun and the other stars'" is "the abstract principle of the cosmos as besouled and cherishing of all sentient actualities"—Hartshorne said: "I have believed in this, with temporary hesitations, almost long as I can remember.[3]

Sometimes Hartshorne referred to his upbringing as "pious but liberal," emphasizing that his father accepted evolution and rejected biblical infallibility. An important ingredient in this pious but liberal upbringing was his parents' decision to send Charles to a boarding school for his high school years. The headmaster, an Episcopalian clergyman, accepted and taught evolutionary theory. Hartshorne, accordingly, grew up seeing science and religion as fully compatible.

His parents were, however, orthodox with regard to Christology and beliefs about immortality, and in these areas differences arose. Reading Matthew Arnold's *Literature and Dogma* at about age seventeen led Hartshorne to reject the resurrection and the supernaturalistic interpretation of Jesus. More generally, Hartshorne said, reading this book broke his "dogmatic slumber": "Any religious belief I could henceforth accept would have to be a philosophical one, with reasons that I could grasp as convincing."[4]

2 Mystical Love of Nature

The loss of his Christian orthodoxy, however, did not leave young Hartshorne bereft of religion, because a religious sensibility of another type had been developing. Due in part to the fact that he grew up (first near Pittsburgh, then near Philadelphia) and went to high school in rural areas, he developed a Wordsworthian feeling for nature. Spending many hours in the woods by himself, Hartshorne focused on Kit Carson and Daniel Boone as two of his heroes.

Hartshorne's first vocational plan resulted from this love of nature, in conjunction with a life-changing event in his second year of high school: Upon awakening from an appendectomy for which he had been given ether, he had vivid visual experiences of landscapes, which led to the desire to become a poet. He read as well as wrote much poetry for the next eight years, being especially influenced by Wordsworth and Shelley.

Another crucial event, at age fifteen or sixteen, was the discovery of *Emerson's Essays*. Besides listing Emerson as one of the "mystical poets" who reinforced his feeling for nature,[5] Hartshorne called Emerson his "first philosophical hero," saying that after reading his book he decided to "trust reason to the end."[6]

Hartshorne's love for philosophical prose would eventually win out over his desire to become a poet, but it would never extinguish his love for nature. When in 1962 Hartshorne was invited to go birding all day by Edgar Kinkaid, the great field naturalist, Kinkaid's aunt suggested that Professor Hartshorne might not want to spend all day with birds. Hartshorne's response: "Philosophy all day long might well be too much, but not wild nature."[7]

Hartshorne's study of ornithology, which began in high school after he discovered a book on birdsong, enabled his love of nature to become concrete and scientific and eventually resulted in his 1973 book, *Born to Sing.*[8]

Hartshorne's first two years of college were at Haverford, where he began thinking about his religious ideas philosophically. The decisive influence on him was the Quaker philosophical mystic Rufus Jones, who started Hartshorne "on the consideration of the meaning of Christian or Judaeo-Christian love."[9]

Under Jones, Hartshorne read *The Problem of Christianity*, by Josiah Royce, who became Hartshorne's "second philosophical hero." His life was changed by Royce's chapter on "Community," which draws on Paul's statement that we are "members one of another," and which saved Hartshorne from the doctrine of enlightened self-interest as our highest ethical motivation.[10]

Also important was Jones' contention that mysticism is a matter of degree, so that all people are aware of God to some extent. Furthermore, Jones had his students read Tolstoy, whose writings persuaded Hartshorne to become a pacifist.[11]

Although this stance did not long survive, it probably influenced his decision, once President Wilson had announced America's entry into the World War, to volunteer as an orderly in an army medical corps in France. This decision, besides allowing Hartshorne to continue his studies and to avoid killing, also led to further decisive experiences.

One night, while lying on deck under the stars during the Atlantic crossing, and after reading a novel by H. G. Wells that suggests a notion of a finite deity, Hartshorne had "close to a mystical experience" while thinking about God.[12]

Wells's view that God is the supermind of humanity, not the spirit of the cosmos as a whole, seemed to Hartshorne be based on a mind-matter dualism separating the human mind from the rest of nature. Hartshorne briefly accepted this view, until his next quasi-mystical experience, perhaps the most decisive one of his life.

One day during his stay in France, while looking at a beautiful landscape, he suddenly saw "into the life of things," gaining a sense of all of nature as alive and expressive of feelings.[13] Recalling Santayana's definition of beauty as "objectified pleasure," he rejected the view that pleasure arises as a purely subjective feeling, which is then projected onto the experienced objects. Pleasure is, rather, "given as in the object. . . . Nature comes to us as constituted by feelings."[14]

Hartshorne would later describe his experience as a "phenomenological testing of the idea of mere unfeeling yet directly given objects of perception," resulting in the conclusion that no such objects are given.[15]

Hartshorne now had a basis in immediate experience for the view of nature suggested by the Romantic poets. With regard to God, this meant that, "if God is, as Wells says, the spirit or supermind of humanity, God may be the supermind of inanimate nature (so-called) as well."[16] The rest of his career would involve developing this twofold idea of God as the soul of a universe constituted by feelings.

3 Panpsychism

After his stint in the medical corps, Hartshorne transferred to Harvard, which was amply suited to help shape his developing philosophy. Hartshorne's rejection of materialism and dualism was reinforced by L. T. Troland, a psychologist who had adopted the panpsychism of the founder of psychophysics, Gustav Fechner.

Under Ralph Barton Perry, Hartshorne studied William James, whose essay "The Dilemma of Determinism" ended Hartshorne's flirtation with psychological determinism.[17] The implications of genuine freedom for theology were laid out by W. E. Hocking: Rejecting divine immutability, Hocking portrayed the future as open even for God.[18]

The two logicians from whom Hartshorne took the most courses, H. M. Sheffer and C. I. Lewis, shaped his determination to bring logical precision into the philosophy of religion.

After four years at Harvard, the latter two as a doctoral student, Hartshorne received a fellowship to spend two years in Europe. Although still taking classes for credit, he wrote his dissertation in little more than a month, during which he experienced the "greatest rush of ideas" in his life.[19]

In this study, "An Outline and Defense of the Argument for the Unity of Being in the Absolute or Divine Good," he developed his panpsychist alternative to dualism and materialism, showing how this view allowed all things to be in God. Prominent are the two philosophers in whom Hartshorne had specialized, Plato and Spinoza, both of whom regarded the universe as the body of God.

In his stay in Europe, during which Hartshorne concentrated on the problem of sensation, he attended lectures primarily by Edmund Husserl and Martin Heidegger. Given Hartshorne's experience in France, through which he had come to see sensation as a form of feeling, he was especially critical of Husserl's phenomenology, because of its dualism between feeling and sensation.[20]

4 The Influence of Whitehead

Upon returning to the States in 1925, Hartshorne became an instructor and research fellow at Harvard. His assignments, besides teaching, were to edit the· papers of Charles Sanders Peirce and to serve as a teaching assistant for Alfred North Whitehead, who had just been appointed to the philosophy faculty. "By sheer luck," wrote Hartshorne, "I was to be intensively exposed, virtually simultaneously, to the thought of perhaps the two greatest philosophical geniuses who ever worked primarily in this country."[21] They both reinforced Hartshorne's panpsychism, and from their combined influence he was led to think of "spontaneity" (Peirce) or "creativity" (Whitehead) as all-pervasive.

It was, however, primarily Whitehead's version of panpsychism that he adopted, thanks to its temporal atomicity and its revolutionary doctrine of "prehension," which Hartshorne considered "one of the greatest intellectual discoveries ever made."[22]

According to the doctrine of temporal atomicity, enduring individuals, such as electrons, atoms, cells, and minds, are not the ultimate units of the world, but are composed of momentary events, each of which prehends its predecessor as well as other prior events. This prehension is a sympathetic feeling of the feelings of the prior experiences. Although the new experience, having its own creative power, is not completely determined by the influences it receives from these prior experiences, it is largely constituted out of these sympathetic feelings of prior feelings.

This doctrine provided Hartshorne the basis for portraying love as the clue to existence. Fundamentally, Hartshorne emphasized, love is sympathy—feeling the feelings of the other with the other. The view that the enduring self is not simply a self-identical substance through time, being instead a temporal society of occasions of experience each of which is largely constituted by its sympathetic feelings of prior events, gave Hartshorne a philosophical basis for regarding his favorite Pauline statement, that we are "members one of another," as rather literally true.[23]

This doctrine means that we are created out of our loves. We do not first have a self, which may then enter into loving relations. "It is our loves that make us anything worth mentioning."[24] Our strongest loves, at least initially, are for our bodily cells: Our sympathetic prehensions of their feelings result in pains and pleasures. We also identify deeply with the feelings of our own prior occasions of experience, so deeply that we tend to take this identification for sheer identity.

But if our identity with our own past, as well as with our body, is only a relative identity rather than a strict one, then what we usually call "self-interest" is already a form of altruism, genuine sympathy for the welfare of others.

Recognition of this fact provided Hartshorne, in turn, the basis for making sense of the second Great Commandment. The usual view, according to which the self is an enduring substance, makes loving my neighbor as myself impossible in principle, because my relation to my self is one of sheer identity and my relation to my neighbor is one of sheer nonidentity. It thereby promotes a doctrine of egoism, according to which we can truly love only ourselves.[25] Accordingly, this "traditional interpretation of 'person' betrays the Gospel ideal."[26]

The social view of the person, by contrast, explains self-love in terms of altruism, thereby showing that we really can, in principle, love other people in the same way that we love ourselves.[27] The importance for Hartshorne of this ethical implication of the social view is revealed in his statement that, on this ground alone, he would not give it up "without the most rigorous proofs of its erroneousness."[28]

Besides explaining enduring individuality, the idea of prehension, as the feeling of prior feelings, accounts for causality (thereby overcoming Hume's problem), time, space, memory, perception, the subject-object relation, the mind-body relation, and the God-world relation. Nine apparently fundamental categories have been reduced to one! Hartshorne refers to this achievement as "the most powerful metaphysical generalization ever accomplished" and "a feat comparable to Einstein's."[29]

Although Hartshorne correctly called Whitehead the "greatest single creator" of this generalization, it was Hartshorne who called attention to its importance. In any case, it is the power of the concept of prehension to make sense of all these categories, showing sympathy or love to be the clue to cosmology and epistemology as well as to religion and ethics, that enabled Hartshorne to flesh out his early intuition that love is the key to existence.[30]

5 Science and Panpsychism

After three years as an instructor at Harvard, Hartshorne joined the philosophy department at the University of Chicago, where he would work out the distinctive emphases of his philosophy. Hartshorne also held a joint appointment with Chicago's Divinity School for more than a decade. Various encounters at the University, in conjunction with his prior ideas, shaped the direction his writing took.

A most important encounter was that with Dorothy Cooper, a musician, who became his wife. Hartshorne attributed his first book, *The Philosophy and Psychology of Sensation*, to her influence, along with the fact that he had been asked to teach aesthetics.[31] In this book he worked out, in relation to the science of psychology, his phenomenological argument that nature as directly intuited is given as feelings, along with his panpsychist argument that we can have a positive conception of "matter" only by conceiving it as consisting in lowly forms of feeling. Physics, accordingly, would be the most primitive branch of comparative psychology.

Hartshorne's panpsychism, which had already been supported by several eminent scientists (Fechner, Troland, Peirce, and Whitehead), received further reinforcement from the man who became his best friend at Chicago and whom he calls "the finest scientific mind I have ever known intimately," the evolutionary biologist Sewall Wright.[32] His friendship with Wright arose after he was included as the one philosopher in the scientific "X Club," to which Hartshorne belonged for 25 years and which gave him a firsthand acquaintance with scientific thinking.

In his next book, *Beyond Humanism*, he argued that in various ways—for example, by showing that the inanimate objects of sensory perception are pseudo-unities, not genuine individuals; by showing that the objects of perception with which we do not sympathize are only indirectly, not directly, intuited; and by pointing to indeterminism in the elementary constituents of nature—science supports panpsychism and thereby "a companionable nature."[33]

We can now "see nature as the pervasively animate and sentient affair Wordsworth (also Shelley) and prescientific peoples saw it as being," Hartshorne said. "That science no longer stands in the way of so doing," he added, "is a cultural fact the learned world has scarcely begun to take in."[34]

6 Panentheism and the Existence of God

This view of a nature that can be loved was articulated not in opposition to, but in support of, a theistic worldview. Hartshorne's argument was that humanism — the idea that the proper object of religious devotion is "humanity considered in its noblest aspirations and capacities"[35] — must give way to "the intellectual, aesthetic, and moral love of nature as the body of God, in all parts having some degree, however slight, of kinship with ourselves, and as a whole immeasurably superior to us, and hence worthy of our highest reverence."[36]

In that book and his next, *Man's Vision of God*, Hartshorne called his position "pantheism," even while attributing freedom to both God and to creatures. In an epilogue to the latter book, however, Hartshorne pointed out that panentheism is a better term, because "it distinguishes God from the 'all' and yet makes him include all."[37]

The key to Hartshorne's panentheism and thereby his theology as a whole, to which all his experience and thought had been leading, is the use of the mind-body relation, understood panpsychistically, as the basic analogue for thinking of the God-world relation. Unlike dualism and materialism, panpsychism makes the mind-body relation intelligible:

> [C]ells can influence our human experience — because they have feelings that we can feel. To deal with the influences of human experience upon cells, one turns this around. We have feelings that cells can feel.[38]

This relation can then be used as the analogue for the God-world relation: The universe is the body of God, and God is the mind or soul of the universe. Because all creatures have feelings, they can all feel God, who, as the "highest level of feeling,"[39] feels their feelings in return. We can thereby understand how God can influence all creatures, including subatomic entities, so as to account for the basic laws of nature as well as human ideals, and how God can in turn know the world, and thereby include it—which is the meaning of panentheism.

The mind-body analogy, furthermore, is the only adequate one, Hartshorne insisted, for understanding the idea that love constitutes the very nature of God. Although traditional Christian theologians used the word "love" in describing the divine nature, "They emptied it of its most essential kernel, the element of sympathy, or the feeling of others' feelings."[40]

A notable reason for this has been the tendency to understand perceptual knowledge in terms of sensory perception. The objects of such perception, being outside the body, are perceived only very indirectly. Using this type of perception as the analogue for divine perceptual knowledge of the world resulted in the idea that God could know the creatures without sympathizing with them. One consequence was the monstrous picture of God as enjoying, or at least indifferently observing, the sufferings of sinners in hell.[41]

As omnipresent, however, God is supposed to be immediately related to all creatures. We have this kind of immediate relation to our bodily members. In this relation, knowledge is sympathy, because in prehending our bodily members, we feel their feelings. This is most obvious in pain (or pleasure), in which we feel pain (or pleasure) because we are sympathetically feeling the pains (or enjoyments) of our bodily cells. (That this is also true in sensation, albeit less obviously, was the burden of Hartshorne's first book.)

Our bodily members, however, are the only "others" with whom we necessarily sympathize. Accordingly, most of our knowledge of others can be devoid of love, because our bodies are very fragmentary portions of reality, so that most "others" are outside them and thereby beyond the range of our direct, sympathetic intuition.

> But suppose all "others" were within the body, as its members; then, since the need of the body is for the flourishing of its

own parts or members, bodily desire and altruism would be coincident.[42]

If God is the soul of the universe, so that God directly prehends all creatures, the necessary goodness of God, meaning God's love for all creatures and desire to promote their welfare, follows naturally.[43]

The mind-body analogy also lies behind Hartshorne's two main reasons for believing in the existence of God: the twofold need for a cosmic source of order and for an everlasting recipient and preserver of value. That these are his two main reasons can be obscured by the fact that Hartshorne has developed several other arguments for God's existence, including the ontological argument, to which he has devoted two books, leading some interpreters to regard it as his main argument. He clearly stated, however, that he had "not used this argument as the way, or even as, by itself, a very good way, to justify belief in God,"[44] and that the arguments from order and value are the two primary ones.[45]

The argument from order to an Orderer depends in part on the fact that, in Hartshorne's panpsychism, the ultimate units of nature have an element of creativity or spontaneity: "Accepting creativity as ultimate category, how is cosmic order possible without a supreme form of creativity, a divine form, to persuade the lesser forms to conform to the minimal requirements of a viable universe?"[46]

We have some insight into how a soul of the universe could account for its order in our own experience:

> Why is it that my cells to a certain extent respond to my wishes or decisions? I am like a little deity in the mind-body system. . . . In this sense deity is the analogically ideal case of what we are as animals. Our conscious feeling or thought is superior to that of our cells; therefore they are somewhat obedient to our imperatives. We persuade them. In Whitehead's Platonic scheme this is what God does to all subjects.[47]

The mind-brain analogy provides a basis for understanding not only divine ordering, but also divine creating, because "experiences" exercise a creative influence upon the development of brain cells."[48] This analogy does not, to be sure, provide a basis for conceiving of creation *ex nihilo*. But Hartshorne had no interest in supporting that view, in part precisely because we have no analogies for it,[49] and in part because it results in an insoluble problem of evil.

The problem of evil, of course, has been one of the main reasons for denying that the world's order points to a Divine Orderer. That problem resulted from the traditional concept of divine omnipotence, according to which God has "the power to determine every detail of what happens in the world."[50] Of this concept of omnipotence, which Hartshorne called "the tyrant ideal of power," he wrote: "No worse falsehood was ever perpetrated."[51] God has perfect power, in the sense of the highest conceivable form of power, but this cannot be the power completely to determine the actions of other individuals, because to be an "individual" is to have some power or freedom of one's own.[52]

Unlike many theologians, Hartshorne did not limit this explanation to evils caused by human beings: Not only human individuals but individuals as such necessarily have some degree of freedom or creativity. This view, Hartshorne explained, "enables us to get rid of the monstrous question, why would a loving God torture (punish or discipline) us with the ills from which we suffer?"[53]

This solution to the problem of evil, Hartshorne stressed, does not mean a "limitation" on God's power, because that way of putting it would suggest that God's power, defined as not all-determining, "fails to measure up to some genuine ideal." His point, instead, is that "omnipotence as usually conceived is a false or indeed absurd ideal."[54] That is, the concept of an individual who could fully determine the actions of other individuals is a self-contradictory concept. The world's evils, accordingly, do not contradict the idea that the world's order points to a Divine Orderer.

Hartshorne's other main basis for believing in God was that, without God's everlasting experience to which we can contribute and from which we can derive a standard of value, there would be no supreme aim around which our lives could be rationally oriented.[55] In part, the issue here is the need for an all-inclusive beneficiary: We presuppose that it is better to relieve the suffering of two or more persons than of only one, and yet, because good is always good for someone, this would be unintelligible apart from an all-inclusive Someone who experiences the greater good.[56]

The other part of the issue is that of immortality: Promoting my own good cannot provide an ultimate meaning for my life, given the fact that I will die. Even living for others is finally inadequate, because this "social immortality," assuming that it is limited to our influences upon other creatures, will also be limited in duration. The answer to these problems might seem to be personal immortality. But literal everlasting life, which would make us as infinite as God is in one respect, is not possible for creatures; existence forevermore, like omnipresence and necessary existence, can be predicated only of God.[57]

The importance of this argument to Hartshorne evidently contributed to his hostility to the idea of life after death. The difference between this idea and that of everlasting life he generally blurred.[58] In any case, serving God in the sense of contributing to the divine experience, primarily by contributing to the good of fellow creatures, is the only inclusive aim that can withstand examination.

Although it may sound like merely an argument for why we should wish that God exists, not for believing that God really does exist, Hartshorne's basic argument here seemed to be that, because we all finally presuppose that life has meaning,[59] and because this presupposition can be true only if God as immortalizer of all our achievements really exists, we all, down deep, believe in God thus conceived. Just as the argument from order draws on the mind's ordering of its body as analogue, this argument from value draws upon the mind's inclusive experience of the multitude of bodily experiences. Both sides are reflected in Hartshorne's statement that "there must . . . be some highest level of feeling from which all the other forms receive directives by which their conflicts are kept within limits, also by which the others can add up to a significant totality."[60]

7 Contributionism and the Nature of God

This idea was of such overwhelming importance to Hartshorne that he spoke of his "religion of contributionism," according to which: "We contribute our feelings to others, and above all to the Universal Recipient of feeling, the One 'to Whom all hearts are open.'"[61]

This religion of contributionism was Hartshorne's way of explicating the Great Commandment, that we love God with all our being. Because of his panentheistic view of the God-world relation, this commandment is not in tension with that to love our neighbors as ourselves, because (Hartshorne said, with an allusion to Matthew 25) we should love all creatures, both ourselves and others, as valuable to God.[62]

Most of Hartshorne's philosophical theology can, in fact, be understood as his attempt to overcome what he saw as the four main obstacles to this religion of contributionism. Three of these have already been discussed: atheism due to the idea that there are no valid arguments for God; atheism based on the problem of evil created by the conventional view of divine power; and the idea of our souls as immortal, which leads us to think in terms of God's everlasting contributions to us instead of ours to God.[63] The fourth obstacle to a religion of contributionism is the idea of divine independence or impassibility, according to which God cannot receive value from the world.

Hartshorne's rejection of this idea, which is implicit in the foregoing, was at the center of his thought about the nature of God. Early in his career at Chicago, Hartshorne was advised by his dean, fellow philosopher Richard McKeon, that he would be unwise to put his energy into philosophy of religion, because it was "less exact" than the other branches of philosophy. It was, however, "precisely this lack of precision" that Hartshorne saw a chance to correct.[64]

The main form this concern took was that of trying to work out an exhaustive list of the logically possible ideas of perfection, or God. One way to argue for a position is to eliminate the other possible positions. But such arguments are usually invalid, because all the other possible views are seldom considered. Many discussions, for example, ask simply whether a "perfect" being exists, taking perfect to be equatable with "absolute." The choices are thereby reduced to two: atheism or classical theism.

However, given the elementary distinction between *all* and *some*, the options are not limited to "absolute in all respects" and "absolute in no respects." There is also the possibility of being "absolute in some respects, relative in others." That this third, usually neglected, option is the truth about God is reflected in the title of one of Hartshorne's most popular books, *The Divine Relativity,* and one of its chapter titles, "God as Absolute, Yet Related to all."

Hartshorne's doctrine of divine relativity involved a version of dipolar theism, according to which God has a relative as well as an absolute aspect or pole. Although several prior thinkers had implied such a distinction (as shown by *Philosophers Speak of God*, which Hartshorne co-edited),[65] Whitehead was the first leading thinker explicitly to enunciate such a position, while it was left to Hartshorne to work out this position more fully.[66]

In Hartshorne's version, God is conceived by analogy with the mind as an enduring individual, meaning a personally ordered society of occasions of experience. The two poles, which Hartshorne calls God's "concrete states" and "abstract essence," are analogous, respectively, to the successive concrete experiences of a person and the abstract character that is exemplified in each such experience. Such a distinction means rejecting the traditional idea of divine "simplicity," according to which there is no difference between God's essence and actuality.

The rejection of that notion of simplicity involved, in turn, a rejection of the idea that God is nontemporal and thereby independent in all respects. On the one hand, the abstract essence of God is completely necessary, eternal, independent, absolute, impassible, and unchanging. Although it is analogous to a human being's abstract character, the divine essence is qualitatively different in the sense that it exists necessarily and eternally, cannot be affected by anything, and does not change in any sense. Because this aspect of God exemplifies the attributes that classical theism ascribed to God as a whole, Hartshorne calls his position "neoclassical theism." The difference implied by the prefix "neo," however, is radical, because those attributes apply to a mere abstraction.

The concrete states of God, which are God as fully actual at any moment, are contingent, temporal, dependent, relative, and changing. The distinction can be illustrated in terms of the distinction between God's *omniscience*, as an abstract characteristic that is exemplified by every divine state or experience, and God's concrete *knowledge* in any such state. God's omniscience, as the capacity to know everything that is knowable at any particular time, is an eternal, necessary, absolute, unchanging characteristic of God, which does not depend upon anything.

But God's concrete knowledge of the world is contingent, insofar as it is knowledge of contingent events, which may or may not have happened. This point presupposes, of course, the idea that worldly events involve an element of spontaneity, so that they are not completely determinable by God or even fully knowable in advance.

Omniscience, accordingly, as the capacity to know everything knowable, does not involve knowledge of the future, beyond whatever abstract aspects of the future are already determined by present forces.

Although some interpreters have thought that this divine dipolarity means that God is perfect in some respects but imperfect in others, that was emphatically not Hartshorne's meaning. He came to speak of "dual transcendence" to stress that the two aspects of God involve two ways of being uniquely excellent.[67]

These two types of perfection involve two kinds of value, those for which a maximal realization is conceivable and those for which it is not.[68] For example, a maximal realization is possible with regard to the capacity for knowledge, because a being could conceivably know everything (then) knowable. There can be no maximal realization of concrete knowledge, however, because there will always be new things to know.

Likewise, there can be a maximal case of goodness: a being whose decisions would be based on sympathetic concern for all beings whatsoever. However, there cannot, the traditional language of "perfect bliss" notwithstanding, be a maximal case of happiness: Further joys, derived from subsequent events, can always enrich any given state of happiness; and, had there been more joy in the world, less agony, the divine happiness would be greater.

The two kinds of perfection are called "absolute" and "relative." God's perfection with regard to those values for which a maximal realization is possible is absolute, meaning "unsurpassable." To say that divine perfection with regard to the other kind of values is "relative" does not mean that God somehow responded less well than God might have; that would be imperfection. Rather, the perfection is relative to a subsequent state of the divine existence. These relative perfections involve surpassability, but only by God in a subsequent state.

With this distinction between two kinds of perfection, the second of which allows the world to contribute value to God, Hartshorne has overcome his "sharpest objection to classical theism," which is "its making God the giver of everything and recipient of nothing."[69]

His revision means that Hartshorne, unlike classical theists, can use the cross as a symbol for divine perfection — that is, for divine love as perfectly responsive to the feelings of all creatures, including their sufferings.[70]

The full development of Hartshorne's doctrine of dual transcendence involved his "logic of ultimate contrasts," which he regarded as "the real center of the system."[71] The idea is that the most general concepts express ultimate contrasts such as necessity and contingency, absoluteness and relativity, independence and dependence, simplicity and complexity, infinity and finitude, timelessness and temporality, being and becoming. The first member of each pair, which alone was attributed to God by classical theism, applies in neoclassical theism to God as merely abstract. It was the one-sidedness of classical theism, involving the "fallacy of misplaced concreteness,"[72] that prevented the God of the philosophers from also being the God of religion.

Hartshorne's contention was that, by beginning with the religious idea of God as love, we can have a doctrine of God that is philosophically intelligible as well.[73] The attribution of these contrasting terms, such as absoluteness and relativity, or eternality and temporality, does not entail paradoxes, because the two attributes apply to different aspects of God, which are not on the same level.

Because the most general concepts come in pairs, the basic issues about reality can be stated in terms of a limited number of options. For example, taking the contrast of necessity and contingency and applying it to God and the world, we can see that there are only sixteen possibilities. Counterintuitive implications eliminate fifteen of these, Hartshorne argued, leaving as the truth the view that God is necessary in some respects and contingent in others, and that the world is contingent in some respects and necessary in others.

The necessity of the world refers not to our particular world, but only to some world or other. The same sixteen options obtain for any of the other contrasts, such as absoluteness and relativity. Hartshorne considered this discovery, which was most thoroughly spelled out in his final book, *The Zero Fallacy*,[74] to be his most important contribution.[75]

8 Conclusion

Hartshorne left Chicago for the philosophy department at Emory University in 1955, then in 1962 went to the University of Texas at Austin, where he became Professor Emeritus in 1978, after which he and Dorothy decided to remain in Austin. When this essay was originally published in 1996, Dorothy had recently died, but Charles, nearly one hundred, was still going strong, having published many books and articles in his old age. The connection between his extensive writing and his religion of contributionism was brought out in a gloss on the scriptural idea that one's life should be a "reasonable, holy, and living sacrifice" to deity. Hartshorne wrote: "If I can inspire multitudes who will never see me in the flesh, then the incense I send up to God will continue to rise anew for many generations."[76]

During the final decade of his life, Hartshorne was honored by a volume in the prestigious *Library of Living Philosophers*, through which he was recognized as one of the great philosophers of the twentieth century. The fact that his is a profoundly Christian philosophy, in which love provides the key to existence, makes this recognition a matter of some importance in the history of Christian theology.

Notes

1   Charles Hartshorne, *Creative Synthesis and Philosophic Method* (Open Court; London: SCM Press, 1970), xviii.

2   Charles Hartshorne, *Omnipotence and Other Theological Mistakes* (State University of New York Press 1984), 14.

3   *Existence and Actuality: Conversations with Charles Hartshorne*, ed. John B. Cobb, Jr., and Franklin I. Gamwell (University of Chicago Press, 1984), 77.

4.   *The Philosophy of Charles Hartshorne*. The Library of Living Philosophers, Vol. 20, ed. Lewis Edwin Hahn (Open Court, 1991), 14.

5   Ibid., 640.

6   Charles Hartshorne, *The Logic of Perfection and Other Essays in Neoclassical Metaphysics* (Open Court, 1962), viii.

7   Charles Hartshorne, *The Darkness and the Light: A Philosopher Reflects Upon His Fortunate Career and Those Who Made It Possible* (State University of New York Press, 1990), 298.

8   Charles Hartshorne, *Born to Sing : Interpretation and World Survey of Bird Song* (Indiana University Press, 1973).

9   Charles Hartshorne, *Omnipotence and Other Theological Mistakes* (State University of New York Press, 1984), 107.

10   *The Philosophy of Charles Hartshorne*, 14.

11   Hartshorne, *The Darkness and the Light*, 120-21.

12   Ibid., 126.

13   *Existence and Actuality*, 167.

14   *The Philosophy of Charles Hartshorne*, 17.

15   Ibid., 691.

16   *The Philosophy of Charles Hartshorne*, 18.

17   Ibid., 38.

18   *Existence and Actuality*, xv; *The Philosophy of Charles Hartshorne*, 21.

19   Hartshorne, *The Darkness and the* Light, 174, 364.

20   *The Philosophy of Charles Hartshorne*, 23.

21   Ibid., 24.

22   *Existence and Actuality*, 124.

23   Hartshorne, *Omnipotence and Other Theological Mistakes*, 106.

24   Ibid., 108.

25   Hartshorne, *The Logic of Perfection*, 16–18.

26   Hartshorne, *Omnipotence and Other Theological Mistakes*, 107.

27   Hartshorne, *Creative Synthesis and Philosophic Method*, 191.

28   Ibid., 198.

29   Hartshorne, *Creative Synthesis and Philosophic Method*, 107, 92.

30   Ibid., xviii.

31 Hartshorne, *The Darkness and the* Light, 22.

32 Ibid., 327; *The Philosophy of Charles Hartshorne*, 31.

33 Charles Hartshorne, *Beyond Humanism: Essays in the New Philosophy of Nature* (Willett, Clark, and Co., 1937), 146, 196, 314, 316.

34 Hartshorne, *The Darkness and the Light*, 378.

35 Hartshorne, *Beyond Humanism*, 2.

36 Ibid., 5.

37 Charles Hartshorne, *Man's Vision of God and the Logic of Theism* (Harper & Row, 1947), 348.

38 Hartshorne, *The Logic of Perfection*, 229.

39 Hartshorne, *The Darkness and the Light*, 375.

40 Hartshorne, *Omnipotence and Other Theological Mistakes*, 29.

41 *The Philosophy of Charles Hartshorne*, 662; Hartshorne, *Creative Synthesis and Philosophic Method*, 263.

42 Charles Hartshorne, *Reality as Social Process: Studies in Metaphysics and Religion* (Free Press; Beacon Press, 1953), 141.

43 *The Philosophy of Charles Hartshorne*, 623.

44 *Existence and Actuality*, 126.

45 *The Philosophy of Charles Hartshorne*, 665.

46 Ibid.

47 Ibid., 649; see also Hartshorne, *Creative Synthesis and Philosophic Method*, 284–85.

48 Hartshorne, *Omnipotence and Other Theological Mistakes*, 60.

49 Ibid., 58.

50 Ibid., 11.

51 Ibid., 11, 18.

52 Hartshorne, *Creative Synthesis and Philosophic Method*, 30.

53 *The Philosophy of Charles Hartshorne*, 676.

54 Hartshorne, *Omnipotence and Other Theological Mistakes*, 17.

55 Hartshorne, *Creative Synthesis and Philosophic Method*, 287; *The*

Philosophy of Charles Hartshorne, 665.

56 Ibid., 289.

57 Hartshorne, *Omnipotence and Other Theological Mistakes,* 35–36.

58 Ibid., 4, 47–49.

59 Charles Hartshorne, *A Natural Theology for Our Time* (Open Court, 1967), 47.

60 Hartshorne, *The Darkness and the Light,* 375.

61 Ibid., 379 (quoting Hartshorne's favorite line from the Anglican prayer book).

62 Hartshorne, *Omnipotence and Other Theological Mistakes,* 107.

63 Charles Hartshorne, *Wisdom as Moderation: A Philosophy of the Middle Way* (State University of New York), 1987), 85–86.

64 *The Philosophy of Charles Hartshorne,* 34.

65 Charles Hartshorne and William L. Reese, eds., *Philosophers Speak of God* (University of Chicago Press, 1953).

66 Ibid., 41.

67 Ibid., 643.

68 Hartshorne, *Man's Vision of God and the Logic of Theism,* 36.

69 *The Philosophy of Charles Hartshorne,* 672.

70 Hartshorne, *Omnipotence and Other Theological Mistakes,* 124.

71 *The Philosophy of Charles Hartshorne,* 630.

72 Hartshorne, *Reality as Social Process,* 124.

73 Ibid., 124.

74 *The Zero Fallacy and Other Essays in Neoclassical Philosophy,* ed. Mohammed Valady (Open Court), 1997.

75 *The Philosophy of Charles Hartshorne,* 656.

76 Hartshorne, *The Logic of Perfection,* 257–58.

Acknowledgments

Chapter 1 is a moderately revised version of "Process Theology," *The Encyclopedia of Christianity*, Book 4, ed. Edwin Fahlbusch et al. (Eerdmans, 2005), 364–69.

Chapter 2 is a slight revision of "Reconstructive Theology," *The Cambridge Companion to Postmodern Theology*, ed. Kevin J. Vanhoozer (Cambridge University Press, 2003), 92–108.

Chapter 3 is a slight revision of "Theism and the Crisis in Moral Theory: Rethinking Modern Autonomy," in *Nature, Truth, and Value: Exploring the Thought of Frederick Ferré*, ed. George Allan and Merle Allshouse (Lexington Books, 2005), 199–220.

Chapter 4 was originally published as "Religious Pluralism," in *Handbook of Process Theology*, ed. Jay McDaniel and Donna Bowman (Chalice Press, 2006), 49–58.

Chapter 5 is a slight revision of "Process Eschatology," in *The Oxford Handbook of Eschatology*, ed. Jerry L. Walls (Oxford University Press, 2007), 295–310.

Chapter 6, "Process Theodicy and Climate Change," scheduled to be published in Jerome Gellman et al., *The History of Evil: From the Mid-20th Century to Today: 1950-2015* (Acumen Publishing, 2017).

Chapter 7 is a significant revision of "Divine Goodness and Demonic Evil," in *Evil and the Response of World Religion*, ed. William Cenkner (Paragon House, 1997), 223–40.

Chapter 8 is a slightly revised version of "Charles Hartshorne," in Donald W. Musser and Joseph L. Price, eds., *Handbook of Christian Theologians* (Abingdon Press, 1996).

Index

Altieri, Charles, 19, 21
anarchy, international (global),
35, 150-51, 152, 153
Apel, Karl-Otto, 30
Arnold, Matthew, 158
Athenagoras, 120
Augustine, Saint, 5, 53, 118, 142,
143

Beardslee, William, 20
Being Itself, 32, 33, 79, 81
Benacerraf, Paul, 44, 45, 46, 56,
57, 59, 60, 61
Berkeley, Bishop, 56
Birch, Charles, 20
Brown, Lester, 113
Buddhism, 7, 11, 27, 70, 76, 78,
81, 82

Calvin, John, 5, 53, 118
Cartesian dualism, 28, 98, 99,
102. *See also* René Descartes.

causation, 4, 24, 26, 28; efficient
and final, 4, 31, 32, 44; mental,
100-01
Center for a Postmodern World,
20
Chomsky, Noam, 114
Christ, Carol, 34
Clement of Alexandria, 120
Cobb, John B., 9, 18-20, 34, 35,
69, 73-74, 81-83, 94, 104, 106
coercive power, 5, 6, 9, 32, 145,
150, 151, 152
common sense, 30, 101
contributionism, 171, 176
Cooper, Dorothy, 165
creatio ex nihilo, 4, 7, 32, 80,
86n47, 118-24, 131, 134, 169
creation out of chaos, 4, 32, 55,
79, 119, 121, 122, 123, 130, 131
creativity, 4-8, 10, 31, 32, 33, 61,
78-81, 130, 132-33, 143, 146,

68546005R00119

Made in the USA
Lexington, KY
14 October 2017